First World War

and Army of Occupation

War Diary

France, Belgium and Germany

25 DIVISION
75 Infantry Brigade
Border Regiment
8th Battalion
26 September 1915 - 30 June 1918

WO95/2251/3

The Naval & Military Press Ltd
www.nmarchive.com
Published in association with The National Archives

Published by

The Naval & Military Press Ltd

Unit 10 Ridgewood Industrial Park,

Uckfield, East Sussex,

TN22 5QE England

Tel: +44 (0) 1825 749494

www.naval-military-press.com

www.nmarchive.com

This diary has been reprinted in facsimile from the original. Any imperfections are inevitably reproduced and the quality may fall short of modern type and cartographic standards.

Contents

Document type	Place/Title	Date From	Date To
Heading	WO95/2251-3		
Heading	25th Division 75th Infy Bde 8th Bn Border Regt Sep 1915-June 1918		
Heading	8th Border Regt Vol, I. Sept & Oct 15		
Miscellaneous	Headquarters 75th Infantry Brigade	04/03/1918	04/03/1918
Miscellaneous			
Miscellaneous	75th Infantry Brigade	05/08/1917	05/08/1917
War Diary	Atdurih At	26/09/1915	26/09/1915
War Diary	Boulogne	27/09/1915	27/09/1915
War Diary	Strazeelle	28/09/1915	28/09/1915
War Diary	Le Bizet	29/09/1915	03/10/1915
War Diary	Right Centre Section of Trenches E, of Ploegstreet	04/10/1915	09/10/1915
War Diary	Ploegstreet	10/10/1915	14/10/1915
War Diary	Right Centre Section of Trenches E of Ploegstreet	15/10/1915	21/10/1915
War Diary	Ploegstreet	22/10/1915	25/10/1915
War Diary	Trenches	26/10/1915	29/10/1915
War Diary	Ploegsteert	30/10/1915	03/11/1915
War Diary	Ploegsteert & Trenches	04/11/1915	04/11/1915
War Diary	Trenches	05/11/1915	09/11/1915
War Diary	Trenches & Ploegsteert	10/11/1915	10/11/1915
War Diary	Ploegsteert	11/11/1915	16/11/1915
War Diary	Trenches	17/11/1915	21/11/1915
War Diary	Trenches & Ploegsteert	22/11/1915	22/11/1915
War Diary	Ploegsteert	23/11/1915	27/11/1915
War Diary	Ploegsteert & Trenches	28/11/1915	28/11/1915
War Diary	Trenches	29/11/1915	30/11/1915
Heading	8th Border Rgt. Vol. 3		
War Diary	Trenches	01/12/1915	02/12/1915
War Diary	Trenches & Ploegsteert	03/12/1915	04/12/1915
War Diary	Ploegsteert	05/12/1915	07/12/1915
War Diary	Ploegsteert & Trenches	08/12/1915	09/12/1915
War Diary	Trenches	10/12/1915	12/12/1915
War Diary	Trenches & Ploegsteert	13/12/1915	17/12/1915
War Diary	Ploegsteert & Trenches	18/12/1915	19/12/1915
War Diary	Trenches	20/12/1915	22/12/1915
War Diary	Trenches & Ploegsteert	23/12/1915	23/12/1915
War Diary	Ploegsteert	24/12/1915	26/12/1915
War Diary	Ploegsteert & Trenches	27/12/1915	31/12/1915
Heading	8th Battn. Border Regiment. January, 1916		
Heading	8th Border Rgt. Vol. 4 Jan 1916		
War Diary	Trenches	01/01/1916	01/01/1916
War Diary	Trenches & Ploegsteert	02/01/1916	06/01/1916
War Diary	Ploegsteert & Trenches	07/01/1916	12/01/1916
War Diary	Trenches & Ploegsteert	13/01/1916	14/01/1916
War Diary	Ploegsteert	15/01/1916	18/01/1916
War Diary	Trenches	19/01/1916	22/01/1916
War Diary	Trenches & Ploegsteert	23/01/1916	23/01/1916
War Diary	Ploegsteert	24/01/1916	26/01/1916
War Diary	La Cheche	27/01/1916	27/01/1916
War Diary	Strazeele	28/01/1916	31/01/1916

Heading	8th Battn. Border Regiment. February 1916		
Heading	8th Border Reg 25th Div. Vol. 5		
War Diary	Strazeele	01/02/1916	29/02/1916
Heading	8th Battn. Border Regiment. March 1916		
War Diary	Strazeele	01/03/1916	09/03/1916
War Diary	Strazeele & Bolinghen	10/03/1916	10/03/1916
War Diary	Bolinghem Nidon	11/03/1916	11/03/1916
War Diary	Nedon	12/03/1916	15/03/1916
War Diary	Nedon Bryan	16/03/1916	23/03/1916
War Diary	Bryas	24/03/1916	31/03/1916
Heading	8th Battn. Border Regiment. April. 1916		
War Diary	Monchy Breton	01/04/1916	20/04/1916
War Diary	Nanchy Breton Trenches	21/04/1916	21/04/1916
War Diary	Trenches	22/04/1916	26/04/1916
Heading	8th Battn. Border Regiment. May.1916		
War Diary	Trenches	27/04/1916	09/05/1916
War Diary	Ecoivres	10/05/1916	19/05/1916
War Diary	Trenches	20/05/1918	20/05/1918
War Diary	Neulle St Vaast	21/05/1918	25/05/1918
War Diary	Trenches	26/05/1916	31/05/1916
Heading	8th Battn. Border Regiment. June 1916		
War Diary	ACQ	01/06/1916	01/06/1916
War Diary	Savy	02/06/1916	13/06/1916
War Diary	Binneutte	14/06/1916	14/06/1916
War Diary	Laquenic be Bmc	15/06/1916	16/06/1916
War Diary	Proville	17/06/1916	17/06/1916
War Diary	Camart	18/06/1916	19/06/1916
War Diary	Doumart	20/06/1916	24/06/1916
War Diary	Talmas	25/06/1916	30/06/1916
Heading	8th Battalion. The Border Regiment. July 1916		
Miscellaneous	The Officer i/c A. G's Office Base	11/08/1916	11/08/1916
War Diary	Fuanille	01/07/1916	01/07/1916
War Diary	Maratinsant Line	02/07/1916	03/07/1916
War Diary	Martinsaart Wood & Aveluy Wood	04/07/1916	12/07/1916
War Diary	Ovillers	13/07/1916	17/07/1916
War Diary	Senlis	18/07/1916	18/07/1916
War Diary	Amplier	19/07/1916	21/07/1916
War Diary	Amplier & Vauchelles	22/07/1916	22/07/1916
War Diary	Vauchelles & Acheux	23/07/1916	23/07/1916
War Diary	Acheux	24/07/1916	25/07/1916
War Diary	Hailey Wood	26/07/1916	31/07/1916
Miscellaneous	75th Inf. Bde.	04/07/1916	04/07/1916
Miscellaneous	8 Borders Vol 6		
Heading	8th Battalion The Border Regiment August 1916		
War Diary	Front Line French Appets Basement Hamel	01/08/1916	05/08/1916
War Diary	Bde Reserve	06/08/1916	09/08/1916
War Diary	Avihon Willers to Warmont Wood	09/08/1916	14/08/1916
War Diary	Warminton Wood & Raincheval	15/08/1916	17/08/1916
War Diary	Forceville	18/08/1916	25/08/1916
War Diary	Trenches	26/08/1916	31/08/1916
Heading	8th Border Regt. September 1916		
War Diary	Trenches & Bouzincourt	01/09/1916	07/09/1916
War Diary	Bouzincourt	08/09/1916	08/09/1916
War Diary	Lillevillers	09/09/1916	09/09/1916
War Diary	Amplier	10/09/1916	11/09/1916
War Diary	Domleger	12/09/1916	25/09/1916

War Diary	Aciphier	26/09/1916	26/09/1916
War Diary	Lealvillers	27/09/1916	30/09/1916
Heading	8th Battn. Border Regiment. October 1916		
War Diary	Onillies	01/10/1916	05/10/1916
War Diary	Trenches	06/10/1916	06/10/1916
War Diary	Curpese Corner	07/10/1916	13/10/1916
War Diary	Criulex Cuner	14/10/1916	14/10/1916
War Diary	Staff Redent	15/10/1916	23/10/1916
War Diary	Gegaincourt	24/10/1916	29/10/1916
War Diary	Meteren	30/10/1916	31/10/1916
Heading	8th Battn. Border Regiment. November 1916		
War Diary	Ponche Nieppe	01/11/1916	02/11/1916
War Diary	Ramsin	03/11/1916	07/11/1916
War Diary	Trenches	08/11/1916	25/11/1916
War Diary	Red Lodge	26/11/1916	30/11/1916
Heading	8th Battn. Border Regiment. December 1916		
War Diary	Red Lodge	01/12/1916	08/12/1916
War Diary	Ploegsteert	09/12/1916	17/12/1916
War Diary	Romarin	18/12/1916	22/12/1916
War Diary	Trenches	23/12/1916	31/12/1916
Miscellaneous	Move Orders	04/12/1916	04/12/1916
War Diary	Trenches Ploegsteert	01/01/1917	08/01/1917
War Diary	Nieppe	09/01/1917	17/01/1917
War Diary	Pont Demene	18/01/1917	22/01/1917
War Diary	Trenches	23/01/1917	31/01/1917
War Diary	Le Bizet & Support Line	01/02/1917	03/02/1917
War Diary	Trenches	04/02/1917	25/02/1917
War Diary	Eecke	26/02/1917	28/02/1917
Miscellaneous	Headquarters 75th. Infantry Brigade.	01/04/1917	01/04/1917
War Diary	Eecke	01/03/1917	05/03/1917
War Diary	Ebblinghem.	06/03/1917	06/03/1917
War Diary	Nortbecourt	07/03/1917	19/03/1917
War Diary	Agquin Ebblinghem Borre	20/03/1917	26/03/1917
War Diary	Outtersteene	27/03/1917	03/04/1917
War Diary	Neuve Eglise	04/04/1917	04/04/1917
War Diary	Wulverghem	05/04/1917	13/04/1917
War Diary	Steent Je	14/04/1917	19/04/1917
War Diary	Pont De Nieppe	22/04/1917	28/04/1917
War Diary	Erquinghem	29/04/1917	30/04/1917
War Diary	Outersteene	01/05/1917	01/05/1917
War Diary	Outtersteene	01/05/1917	09/05/1917
War Diary	Steent-Je	10/05/1917	14/05/1917
War Diary	La Creche	15/05/1917	28/05/1917
War Diary	Ravelsburg	29/05/1917	02/06/1917
War Diary	Pioneer Camp Neuve Eglise	03/06/1917	06/06/1917
War Diary	Messines Ridge	07/06/1917	08/06/1917
War Diary	Neuve Eglise	09/06/1917	12/06/1917
War Diary	Messines	13/06/1917	16/06/1917
War Diary	De Kennebeg	17/06/1917	22/06/1917
War Diary	Sec Bois Merville St Hilaire	23/06/1917	25/06/1917
War Diary	Erny St Julien	26/06/1917	07/07/1917
War Diary	Steenbecque	08/07/1917	08/07/1917
War Diary	Winnipeg Camp Ouderdom	09/07/1917	22/07/1917
War Diary	Reninghelst Staging Area 'A'	23/07/1917	30/07/1917
War Diary	Belgian Chateau Area	31/07/1917	31/07/1917
War Diary	Bellewarde Farm	01/08/1917	05/08/1917

War Diary	Railway Wood	06/08/1917	07/08/1917
War Diary	Bellewarde Farm	08/08/1917	09/08/1917
War Diary	Winnipeg	10/08/1917	11/08/1917
War Diary	Westhoek	12/08/1917	12/08/1917
War Diary	Dominion Camp	13/08/1917	16/08/1917
War Diary	Swan Chau	17/08/1917	17/08/1917
War Diary	Godewearsveldt	18/08/1917	20/08/1917
War Diary	Steenvorde	21/08/1917	01/09/1917
War Diary	Dominion Camp	02/09/1917	02/09/1917
War Diary	Chau Segard	03/09/1917	05/09/1917
War Diary	Front Line (in Frist of Hooge)	06/09/1917	09/09/1917
War Diary	Ch Au Segard	10/09/1917	10/09/1917
War Diary	Winnipeg Cp	11/09/1917	12/09/1917
War Diary	Pradelles	13/09/1917	13/09/1917
War Diary	Steenbecque	14/09/1917	14/09/1917
War Diary	Marles-Lez-Mines	15/09/1917	26/09/1917
War Diary	Nouex-Les-Mines	27/09/1917	28/09/1917
War Diary	Cite Calonne	29/09/1917	02/10/1917
War Diary	Noeux Le Mines	03/10/1917	04/10/1917
War Diary	Cuinchy Support	05/10/1917	11/10/1917
War Diary	La Bassee	12/10/1917	18/10/1917
War Diary	Le Preol	19/10/1917	23/10/1917
War Diary	Trenches Canal Sector La Bassee	24/10/1917	29/10/1917
War Diary	In Support Pont Fixe	30/10/1917	14/11/1917
War Diary	La Bassee Canal Sector Front Line	05/11/1917	10/11/1917
War Diary	Le Preol	11/11/1917	16/11/1917
War Diary	La Bassee Canal Sector Front Line	17/11/1917	22/11/1917
War Diary	Pont Fixe	23/11/1917	27/11/1917
War Diary	Annezin Burbure Erny St Jolien	28/11/1917	30/11/1917
Heading	75th Inf Bde Appendix II	10/11/1917	11/11/1917
Miscellaneous	Report Upon Raid on Enemy Trenches by 8th Bn. Border Regt.	11/11/1917	11/11/1917
War Diary	25th Division G.S. 238	12/11/1917	12/11/1917
Miscellaneous	25th Division 'G'	11/11/1917	11/11/1917
War Diary	25th Division No. G.S. 238	10/11/1917	10/11/1917
Miscellaneous	Reference Brigade Order No. 206	10/11/1917	10/11/1917
Miscellaneous	25th Division No. G.S. 238/A	09/11/1917	09/11/1917
Miscellaneous	Reference Brigade Order No. 206	09/11/1917	09/11/1917
Miscellaneous	25th Division G.S. 238	09/11/1917	09/11/1917
Miscellaneous	No. 4 Special Company R.E. Operation Order No. 104	08/11/1917	08/11/1917
Miscellaneous	D Special Coy RE Operation Order No. 31	08/11/1917	08/11/1917
Miscellaneous	O.C. 112th Brigade R.F.A.		
Miscellaneous	Amendments to 75th Infantry Brigade Order No. 206	08/11/1917	08/11/1917
Miscellaneous	25th Division No. G.S. 238	08/11/1917	08/11/1917
Operation(al) Order(s)	75th Infantry Brigade Order No. 206/1	07/11/1917	07/11/1917
Miscellaneous	A Form Messages And Signals.	07/11/1917	07/11/1917
Miscellaneous	25th Division	07/11/1917	07/11/1917
Miscellaneous	C Form. Messages And Signals.	07/11/1917	07/11/1917
Operation(al) Order(s)	75th Infantry Brigade Order No. 206	06/11/1917	06/11/1917
Miscellaneous	C Form Messages And Signals.	06/11/1917	06/11/1917
Miscellaneous	25th Division No. G.S. 238	06/11/1917	06/11/1917
Heading	Cover for Documents. Nature of Enclosures. Movements Concentration Method of moving by train and bus Rules for Franching Arty S.A.A. Sections of Divl Amn Columns		
War Diary	Erny St Julien	01/12/1917	04/12/1917

War Diary	Gomecourt Rocquigny	05/12/1917	08/12/1917
War Diary	Rocquigny Beugnaire	09/12/1917	16/12/1917
War Diary	Beugnatre	17/12/1917	20/12/1917
War Diary	Lagnicourt	21/12/1917	26/12/1917
War Diary	Vaulx-Vraucourt	27/12/1917	31/12/1917
War Diary	Vraucourt	01/01/1918	01/01/1918
War Diary	Beugnatre	02/01/1918	13/01/1918
War Diary	Lagnicourt	14/01/1918	31/01/1918
War Diary	Beugnatre	01/02/1918	06/02/1918
War Diary	Lagnicourt	07/02/1918	12/02/1918
War Diary	Logeast Camp	13/02/1918	28/02/1918
Heading	8th Battalion The Border Regiment March 1918		
War Diary	Logeast Camp Achiet Area	01/03/1918	12/03/1918
War Diary	Savoy Camp Achiet Area	13/03/1918	21/03/1918
War Diary	Vaulx-Morchies Line	22/03/1918	22/03/1918
War Diary	Savoy Camp	23/03/1918	23/03/1918
War Diary	Behagnies Sadagnies Lane	24/03/1918	24/03/1918
War Diary	Logeast Wood	25/03/1918	25/03/1918
War Diary	Puisieux Au Mont	26/03/1918	26/03/1918
War Diary	Couin	27/03/1918	27/03/1918
War Diary	Puchevillers	28/03/1918	28/03/1918
War Diary	Vacquerie	29/03/1918	31/03/1918
Heading	8th Battalion The Border Regiment April 1918		
War Diary	Dewaersvelde Prte-Pyp Camp	01/04/1918	01/04/1918
War Diary	Marin Camp	02/04/1918	04/04/1918
War Diary	Touquet Sector	05/04/1918	10/04/1918
War Diary	Oosthove Fme.	11/04/1918	11/04/1918
War Diary	Le Rossignol		
War Diary	Connaught Road Korte Pyp	12/04/1918	12/04/1918
War Diary	Neuve Eglise	13/04/1918	14/04/1918
War Diary	Koudokot Mont Des Cats	15/04/1918	15/04/1918
War Diary	La Levrette	16/04/1918	17/04/1918
War Diary	Les Cats	18/04/1918	20/04/1918
War Diary	Vox Vrie Poperinghe	21/04/1918	24/04/1918
War Diary	Hougraaf Cabaret	25/04/1918	25/04/1918
War Diary	Reninghelst	26/04/1918	26/04/1918
War Diary	Line	27/04/1918	29/04/1918
War Diary	La Clytte	30/04/1918	30/04/1918
War Diary	Kortepyp Romarin	03/04/1918	03/04/1918
War Diary	Romarin	04/04/1918	09/04/1918
War Diary	Le Touquet Oosthove	10/04/1918	10/04/1918
War Diary	Le Bizet Oosthove	10/04/1918	11/04/1918
War Diary	Oosthove	11/04/1918	11/04/1918
War Diary	Rossignol	11/04/1918	11/04/1918
War Diary	Connaught Road	11/04/1918	12/04/1918
War Diary	Neuve Eglise	13/04/1918	15/04/1918
War Diary	Mont Des Cats	16/04/1918	16/04/1918
War Diary	La Levrette		
War Diary	Mont Des Cats	18/04/1918	19/04/1918
War Diary	La Clytte	01/05/1918	03/05/1918
War Diary	St Eloi Cabt L 29 A 10.20	04/05/1918	04/05/1918
War Diary	Wylder	05/05/1918	09/05/1918
War Diary	Train	10/05/1918	10/05/1918
War Diary	Fismes	11/05/1918	11/05/1918
War Diary	Courville	12/05/1918	23/05/1918
War Diary	Romain Camp	24/05/1918	24/05/1918

War Diary	Ventelay	26/05/1918	27/05/1918
War Diary	Roocy		
Miscellaneous			
War Diary	Roocy	27/05/1918	27/05/1918
Miscellaneous			
War Diary	Roocy	27/05/1918	27/05/1918
Miscellaneous			
War Diary	Roocy	27/05/1918	27/05/1918
Miscellaneous			
War Diary	La Raite	27/05/1918	28/05/1918
Miscellaneous	Romain		
Miscellaneous			
War Diary	Lestenteaux	28/05/1918	28/05/1918
War Diary	Courville		
War Diary	Crogny		
Miscellaneous			
War Diary	Romigny	29/05/1918	30/05/1918
Miscellaneous			
War Diary	Crogny	28/05/1918	28/05/1918
War Diary	Aougny	29/05/1918	29/05/1918
War Diary	Romigny		
Miscellaneous			
War Diary	Romigny	30/05/1918	30/05/1918
War Diary	Nappes	31/05/1918	31/05/1918
Miscellaneous			
War Diary	Nappes	31/05/1918	31/05/1918
Miscellaneous			
Heading	War Diary Poyser's Battalion (8th Border Regt. & 9th L.N. Lancs.) June 1918 Volume 33		
War Diary	Nappes	01/06/1918	18/06/1918
War Diary	Nappes Germaine	18/06/1918	18/06/1918
War Diary	St Loup	19/06/1918	22/06/1918
War Diary	Connantray	23/06/1918	23/06/1918
War Diary	Haussimont	24/06/1918	25/06/1918
War Diary	Sommesous	26/06/1918	26/06/1918
War Diary	Hesdin	27/06/1918	27/06/1918
War Diary	Embry	28/06/1918	29/06/1918
War Diary	Map Soissons	01/06/1918	06/06/1918
War Diary	Chalons Sheet	07/06/1918	07/06/1918
War Diary	Beaunay	08/06/1918	08/06/1918
War Diary	Reuyes	09/06/1918	16/06/1918
War Diary	Ref. Map Arcis	17/06/1918	17/06/1918
War Diary	Gaye	18/06/1918	20/06/1918
War Diary	St Loup	21/06/1918	30/06/1918
War Diary	Embry	29/06/1918	30/06/1918

25TH DIVISION
75TH INFY BDE

8TH BN BORDER REGT
SEP 1915-~~MAY~~ JUNE 1918

To ~~50 DIV.~~
~~25 Composite Bde~~
~~DISBANDED JULY 1918~~

DISBANDED

25th Division

75th Bde

121/7608

8th Border Regt
Vol: I

Sept. & Oct. 15

Sep '15
May '18

I.N.
8 sheets

ORDERLY ROOM
8th (Service) Battalion
THE BORDER REGIMENT.
No. 586 R
Date 4/3/18

~~Officer i/c~~
Headquarters
~~Infantry Section No.6,~~
75th Infantry Brigade
~~G.H.Q. 3rd Echelon,~~

~~Base.~~

Herewith War Diary for the month of February, 1918, receipt of which please acknowledge.

CWH Birt

Lieut. Colonel,

4th March, 1918. Commanding 8th Bn. Border Regiment.

NATIONAL

(6424) Wt. 25891/.68 3,000

Officer i/c

Infantry Section No.3,

G.H.Q. 3rd.Echelon,

B.E.F.

Herewith War Diary for the month of February,1916,
receipt of which please acknowledge.

Lieut.Colonel,

4th.March,1916. Commanding 4th.Bn.Border Regiment.

75th Infantry Brigade
Transport Lines.

Herewith War Diary for the month of June receipt of which please acknowledge.

A. W. Reade Captain
for Lieut. Col.
Commandg. 8th Border Regt

5.8.17

Instructions regarding War Diaries and Intelligence Summaries are contained in F. S. Regs., Part II. and the Staff Manual respectively. Title pages will be prepared in manuscript.

WAR DIARY
or
INTELLIGENCE SUMMARY.
(Erase heading not required.)

(1)

Army Form C. 2118.

Place	Date	Hour	Summary of Events and Information	Remarks and references to Appendices
Aldershot	26-9-15	6 PM	Left at 6 PM in two troop trains for Folkestone and Boulogne. Reached Boulogne, disembarked and marched to rest camp about 2 miles out arrived there about 1 AM. Iron rations issued that morning	
Boulogne	27-9-15	9 AM	Left camp at 9, and marched to station, entrained for Hazebrouck, proceeded slowly by rail to that place, detrained at 4 PM, and marched to Strazeele, and billets were found there for the night about 8 PM	
Strazeele	28-9-15	8 AM	Left Strazeele by motor lorries and reached Nieppe about 1.30 PM, and marched to Le Bizet, where billets were found by the Gendarmes for the Batt.	
Le Bizet	29-9-15	8 AM	Three platoons were sent to the trenches that evening under platoon officers for instructional purposes with the 48th Canadian Highlanders who were holding the trenches. All Company Commanders visited the trenches that day	
" "	30-9-15	8 AM	D Company (4 platoons) proceeded to the trenches at 6 PM that evening, relieving the three platoons already there	
" "	1-10-15	8 AM	One platoon from A. B. and C Cos proceeded to the trenches that night at 6 P.M., relieving D Co.	
" "	2-10-15	8 AM	Another platoon from A B and C Cos relieved those already in the trenches at 6.30 PM. One Lance Corp of B Co was shot returning from a listening post on the night of the 1st.	

2353 Wt. W2544/1454 700,000 5/15 D. D. & L. A.D.S.S./Forms/C. 2118.

Instructions regarding War Diaries and Intelligence Summaries are contained in F. S. Regs., Part II. and the Staff Manual respectively. Title pages will be prepared in manuscript.

WAR DIARY
or
INTELLIGENCE SUMMARY.
(Erase heading not required.)

(2)

Army Form C. 2118.

Place	Date	Hour	Summary of Events and Information	Remarks and references to Appendices
Le Bizet	3.10.15	8 AM.	Orders received to go into the trenches that night, billets were vacated, and transport removed all baggage. Left for trenches at 6.20 P.M., marching by platoons. The entire handing over was completed by 9 P.M., and 48th Canadians vacated trenches.	
Right centre section of trenches E of ~~[illegible]~~ PLOEGSTREET	4.10.15	8 AM	A good deal of firing at night, and sniping by the Germans. Casualties one man killed about 6.30 AM, one slightly wounded by shell fire. Repairing of parapets being done, and revetting in communication trench, which was damaged by rain [?]. Artillery observation post found out by enemy.	
" "	5.10.15	8 AM	Much less firing, but a good deal of sniping on the German side, who seem very active at daylight and in the afternoon. Two Germans were seen, one wearing black spiked helmet, the other soft round dark blue cap. Work continued in repairing parapets, and strengthening trenches. Latrines inspected and cleared. Three or four shells came into A Co's trenches, and Convent [?] again shelled.	
" "	6.10.15	8 P.M	A noisy night and a good deal of sniping. Two machine guns opposite C Co on our left were very active. The Co Comdr [?] informed artillery, and with 3 or 4 rounds the machine guns were completely silenced, the range being perfect, and the machine guns are believed to be knocked out, as observed from the trenches. Very little firing from our lines, silence being maintained. Repairs to trenches carried out all day under supervision of R E officers.	

2353 Wt. W2544/1454 700,000 5/15 D. D. & L. A.D.S.S./Forms/C. 2118.

WAR DIARY

or

INTELLIGENCE SUMMARY.

(*Erase heading not required.*)

Army Form C. 2118.

(3)

Instructions regarding War Diaries and Intelligence Summaries are contained in F. S. Regs., Part II. and the Staff Manual respectively. Title pages will be prepared in manuscript.

Place	Date	Hour	Summary of Events and Information	Remarks and references to Appendices
Right centre section of British trenches E of PLOEGSTREET	7.10.15	8 P.M	A good deal of sniping at night. Repairs to trenches continue under R.E. officer's supervision	
" "	8.10.15	8 P.M	A quieter night. Our snipers believed to have accounted for two of the enemy, one sniper and one man at work. Repairs go on as usual.	
" "	9.10.15	8 P.M	A quiet night. Relief completed by 8 P.M., and our Co's occupy the farms where the X Cheshires were in billets.	
PLOEGSTREET	10.10.15	8 P.M	General cleaning up of billets.	
" "	11.10.15	8 P.M	Physical drill in morning. Short route marches. B Co furnished fatigue on second line trenches.	
" "	12.10.15	"	Physical drill, route marching, improving trenches near billets. Baths commenced	
" "	13.10.15	"	D Co furnished fatigue. At 1.30 P.M all second line trenches manned till 7.30 P.M. while guns bombarded enemy's trenches. No casualties.	
" "	14.10.15		Drills as usual and fatigue party. Church of England services carried out in Co's quarters in rotation.	

2353 Wt. W2544/1454 700,000 5/15 D. D. & L. A.D.S.S./Forms/C. 2118.

Instructions regarding War Diaries and Intelligence Summaries are contained in F. S. Regs., Part II. and the Staff Manual respectively. Title pages will be prepared in manuscript.

WAR DIARY
or
INTELLIGENCE SUMMARY.
(Erase heading not required.)

Army Form C. 2118.

(4)

Place	Date	Hour	Summary of Events and Information	Remarks and references to Appendices
Right-Centre Section of trenches E of PLOEGSTREET	15.10.15	8 P.M.	Relieved 8 Cheshires in the trenches. Relief completed by 7 P.M., and trenches handed over.	
" "	16.10.15	8 P.M.	A quiet night. Some shelling in the afternoon in reply to our guns, three shells dropped close to our communication trench, and some others near Lancashire support farm. No damage done. A clear night	
" "	17.10.15	"	Enemy inactive. At night they turned a machine gun on to our communication trench, and tram line. It is evidently well marked, but they just missed the ration party on their way up	
" "	18.10.15	"	The Germans shelled a good deal to-day, both in the morning and afternoon, and inflicted some casualties amongst working parties, especially at Le Touquet Berthe. One casualty amongst the Patrol party in front of our lines at night, Pte Walker, shot thro the arm.	
	19.10.15	"	A little more firing at night, the enemy shelled the trenches a little in the morning, and two casualties from shrapnel, L C Browne, severely wounded in lung, and L C Bell wounded, both of C Co. All work proceeding under direction of R E officers as usual.	
	20.10.15	"	A noisy night, much more firing on German side, apparently due to new reliefs. Capt. McCullagh severely wounded in the leg, putting up wire about 5 AM. Another casualty in B Co the same night. A quiet day, and work proceeded as usual. Hope we have located a German Battery which has been shelling our trenches, and informed the artillery.	

#353 Wt. W2544/1454 700,000 5/15 D. D. & L. A.D.S.S./Forms/C. 2118.

Instructions regarding War Diaries and Intelligence Summaries are contained in F. S. Regs., Part II. and the Staff Manual respectively. Title pages will be prepared in manuscript.

WAR DIARY
or
INTELLIGENCE SUMMARY.
(Erase heading not required.)

Army Form C. 2118.

(5)

Place	Date	Hour	Summary of Events and Information	Remarks and references to Appendices
" "	21.10.15	8 P.M.	A quiet night. Heard of Capt McCullagh's death at No 2 clearing station from collapse. Relief was completed by 5 P.M., and stores and trenches handed over to X battalion	
PLOEGSTREET	22.10.15	"	General cleaning up	
" "	23.10.15	"	A & B Co's on fatigues. C Co went to baths. Memorial service held for Capt McCullagh [illegible] and C Co at 5 P.M.	
" "	24.10.15	"	C & D Co's on fatigue. Divine service for A & B Co's	
" "	25.10.15	"	Relieved X battalion in the trenches. A very wet day and part of communication trench between 1875 farm and Batt H.Q. impassable, owing to walls falling in. Relief completed at 4.30, and trenches handed over.	
Trenches	26.10.15	"	A fine day, and several aeroplanes. One man slightly wounded by shrapnel from anti-aircraft guns and another by a German shell. A quiet day, repairs carried on all day	
" "	27.10.15	"	A quiet day. Two officers and 65 men went to attend the review at Bailleul. Work proceeded as usual. Communication trench between Lawrence Farm and 1875 farm still impassable, and from Lawrence farm to Lancashire Support farm only kept open by pumping.	
"	28.10.15	"	A very quiet night, and wet day. Much work to be done, owing to walls falling in where not revetted	

2353 Wt. W2544/1454 700,000 5/15 D. D. & L. A.D.S.S./Forms/C. 2118.

Army Form C. 2118.

(6)

Instructions regarding War Diaries and Intelligence Summaries are contained in F. S. Regs., Part II. and the Staff Manual respectively. Title pages will be prepared in manuscript.

WAR DIARY
or
INTELLIGENCE SUMMARY.

(Erase heading not required.)

Place	Date	Hour	Summary of Events and Information	Remarks and references to Appendices
Trenches	29.10.15	5 P.M.	A quiet night. Communication trenches again blocked in places by water, and walls falling in. Howitzer fired over our D Co this morning on earthwork. One man S.W. Borderers killed and 5 men of D Co wounded by shell dropping in cook house of D Co. Relief carried out in afternoon by 2nd S Lan Regt. Relief completed by 5 P.M., and trenches handed over.	
Ploegsteert	30.10		Men resting after tour in Trenches. The shell which wounded the men in the Cook house yesterday appears to have been fired by the Germans from a captured French gun from a pt. N of Messines; this was the conclusion arrived at by Brig. Gen. Bethell C.R.A.	
Ploegsteert	31.10		B Company were away nearly all day working with the engineers, improving communication trenches. D Company proceeded to Ploegsteert Wood to gather firewood. The remaining two Companies improved trenches at their own billets.	

3/11/15.

[signature] Col.
Comdg. 8th Border Regiment

8353 Wt. W2544/1454 700,000 5/15 D. D. & L. A.D.S.S./Forms/C. 2118.

XXV

WAR DIARY
or
INTELLIGENCE SUMMARY.
(Erase heading not required.)

Army Form C. 2118.

8th Bn Border Regt

Nov. 1

Instructions regarding War Diaries and Intelligence Summaries are contained in F. S. Regs., Part II. and the Staff Manual respectively. Title pages will be prepared in manuscript.

Place	Date	Hour	Summary of Events and Information	Remarks and references to Appendices
Ploegsteert	Nov 1st		On account of the inclement weather very little was done. A Company sent 1 officer and 100 men to work under the R.E. These men were employed in reconstructing "NORFOLK AVENUE". This communication trench requires a good deal of repairing. The remaining Companies improved the defences in the vicinity of their billets. Quiet day.	
Ploegsteert	2nd		The weather again was very bad, and great difficulty was experienced in getting any satisfactory work done. Parties were sent out to gather wood. C & D Companies supplied large working parties for the R.E. Quiet day.	
Ploegsteert	3rd		A slight improvement in the weather. 3 officers & 200 men were detailed for duty with the R.E. These were again employed in the communication trenches.	
Ploegsteert & Trenches	4th	x	The Battn relieved the 2nd S Lancashire Regt in the trenches. The relief was carried out earlier than intended on account of the clear day. The trenches were in a bad state owing to the continual rain. The [illegible] of the centre section of the line were 2 feet under water. The support trenches which had to be brought back to the Convent farm east of Battn Head Quarters. The advanced dressing station was also flooded. Very little sniping while the relief was being carried out.	
Trenches	5th		A fine day with a little rain. There was hardly any sniping on either side. 2 men Pte Donnelly and Pte Broadbent both of A Company were wounded, both were hit by the same bullet. The post was [illegible] this being a tall chimney. Every available man was employed in repairing damage to the trenches. Pumps were employed to rid the trenches of water. During the night the enemy snipers were fairly active.	L. N. 6 sheets

2353 Wt. W2544/1454 700,000 5/15 D. D. & L. A.D.S.S./Forms/C. 2118.

Instructions regarding War Diaries and Intelligence Summaries are contained in F. S. Regs., Part II. and the Staff Manual respectively. Title pages will be prepared in manuscript.

WAR DIARY
or
INTELLIGENCE SUMMARY.
(Erase heading not required.)

Army Form C. 2118.

Place	Date	Hour	Summary of Events and Information	Remarks and references to Appendices
Trenches	Nov 6th		A very quiet day. The fog was too thick to allow of much sniping. A fairly hard frost in the early hours of the morning. The whole Battn was engaged in improving and repairing the front line trenches and communication trenches. Nothing of importance occurred during the day.	
	7th		Again a quiet day on account of fog. Good progress was made in repairing parapets and communication trenches. Unfortunately Pte Tongston of B Company was killed while repairing parados. Towards evening the enemy's machine guns was active in front of A Company holding the centre section of our line. Our humour tag during the day was one pheasant	
	8th		A distinct improvement in the weather, many of the trenches have been almost emptied of water. The enemy's artillery was particularly active about 11.30 am. Their attention were particularly directed to D Company holding the right of our line. Unfortunately two of our men were hit but neither dangerously. About 4.30 pm our artillery retaliated. The complement also our machine guns were active. At 3.30 pm Pte Dixon of A Company was killed he was working at the support trench	
	9th	×	A quiet day, nothing of importance occurred. Col Spurrell of the 13th Sussex was attached to us for a few days to enable him to visit the trenches. A screen along the tram line was practically completed.	

£353 Wt. W2544/1454 700,000 5/15 D. D. & L. A.D.S.S./Forms/C. 2118.

Army Form C. 2118.

Instructions regarding War Diaries and Intelligence Summaries are contained in F. S. Regs., Part II. and the Staff Manual respectively. Title pages will be prepared in manuscript.

WAR DIARY
or
INTELLIGENCE SUMMARY.

(Erase heading not required.)

Place	Date Nov	Hour	Summary of Events and Information	Remarks and references to Appendices
Trenches & Ploegsteert	10th		The day passed quietly, there was very little sniping but the enemy artillery was fairly active. At 4 pm the relief of the Battn by the 2nd S Lancashire Regt took place.	
Ploegsteert	11th		The Battn rested in billets; during the day all the Companies had baths at Pont de Nieppe and the 25th Divisional bath at Nieppe. The day was fine and our artillery was particularly active. The enemy's reply to this was weak. An aeroplane descended in rear of Soyer Farm, this was a Belgian aeroplane.	
"	12th		Very wet day, detachments from all companies were sent out to assist the R.E. in repairing and reconstructing trenches. A few shells were fired on Ploegsteert at 6.30 pm no damage.	
"	13th		Again a wet day. The usual fatigues were sent out. The enemy's artillery was more active during the evening the enemy again shelled Ploegsteert and the vicinity. One shell penetrated the roof of the stable at Bde H.Q and a few dropped close to the Battn H.Q	
"	14th		A fine and fairly clear day. Church service was held at Soyer Farm. A B & D Companies were supplying the fatigues for the R.E. wiring parties were sent to Caen [illegible] wiring along 12th & 13th.	
"	15th		A quiet day, sniping at the working parties was indulged in by the enemy and we had one casualty Pte Dunney of A Coy who was rather seriously wounded by a bullet in the face.	
"	16th		The Battn relieved the 2nd Batt S Lancashire Regt in the trenches. C Company on right of line A Company in centre and B on the left. D Company in reserve at Lancashire Support Farm. Our artillery very active. No casualties reported.	

2353 Wt. W2544/1454 700,000 5/15 D. D. & L. A.D.S.S./Forms/C. 2118.

Army Form C. 2118.

Instructions regarding War Diaries and Intelligence Summaries are contained in F. S. Regs., Part II. and the Staff Manual respectively. Title pages will be prepared in manuscript.

WAR DIARY
or
INTELLIGENCE SUMMARY.
(*Erase heading not required.*)

Place	Date	Hour	Summary of Events and Information	Remarks and references to Appendices
Trenches	Nov 17th		About 2.30 am the artillery on our left very active. This was in the Canadian sector. This was a demonstration on the part of the Canadians. The trenches still very wet and the centre support line still impassable.	
"	18th		A great deal of difficulty was caused by a considerable rise in the water during the night. The section held by A Coy at 106 was particularly bad. Two pumps were kept hard at work all day to cope with this. The support trenches in this sector had to be abandoned. [illegible] of D Coy was wounded in the head while in the observation post at the Convent.	
	19th		A hard frost during the night and early hours of morning. This caused considerable damage to our parapets. B Coy had difficulty in ridding section 112 of the water. Artillery fire was fairly active on both sides. Unfortunately C Coy had two men hit by our own shells fired from [illegible] battery. They were [illegible].	
	20th		There was a considerable decrease in the water level in both the sections occupied by B Coy and A Coy. The communication trench near Convent was drained of water. Sniping was more active along the whole sector. Night patrolling by [illegible] resulted in the find of a considerable quantity of [illegible] ammunition, equipment etc. Also [illegible]	
	21st		[illegible]. The [illegible] was particularly good. The work of repairing the trenches was steadily carried on. [illegible] A Coy was [illegible] slightly during the afternoon. No 102 trench reported [illegible] machine guns were firing at their trench.	

2353 Wt. W2544/1454 700,000 5/15 D. D. & L. A.D.S.S./Forms/C. 2118.

Instructions regarding War Diaries and Intelligence Summaries are contained in F. S. Regs., Part II. and the Staff Manual respectively. Title pages will be prepared in manuscript.

Army Form C. 2118.

WAR DIARY
or
INTELLIGENCE SUMMARY.
(Erase heading not required.)

Place	Date 1915	Hour	Summary of Events and Information	Remarks and references to Appendices
Trenches & Ploegsteert	22nd		Our relief was carried out by the 2nd Batt S Lancashire Regt in cold and misty weather without any casualties. The relief was completed before dark. During the morning A Company [illegible] had 3 men hit. Pte [illegible] was killed, bullet wound in head. Pte Irvin was wounded in the hand & Pte Ratcliffe in the neck. The last one was of a serious nature. The usual work of repairs and drainage were carried out during the morning.	
Ploegsteert	23rd		A very misty morning. About 11am the enemy dropped a few shells to the North of Ploegsteert. Sgt Hodgson of D Company was wounded in the stomach by a stray bullet near [illegible] Farm ~~[illegible]~~. The Companies had a day in billets and went to [illegible] for hot baths	
"	24th		A B & C Companies were out all day working in parties under the supervision of the R E. A [illegible] day.	
	25th		B C & D companies were out working for the R E. The enemy's artillery were more active than usual and about 40 shells were fired into Ploegsteert during the morning. There were no casualties.	
	26th		A very [illegible] day the usual fatigues took place. A little snow and hail in the morning, a cold day. One man slightly wounded by splinter of shell	
	27th		The enemy shelled Ploegsteert in the morning and also searched for our batteries near [illegible] Farm where A Coy is billeted. One shell burst over the farm but little damage done.	

2353 Wt. W2544/1454 700,000 5/15 D. D. & L. A.D.S.S./Forms/C. 2118.

Army Form C. 2118.

Instructions regarding War Diaries and Intelligence Summaries are contained in F. S. Regs., Part II. and the Staff Manual respectively. Title pages will be prepared in manuscript.

WAR DIARY
or
INTELLIGENCE SUMMARY.
(Erase heading not required.)

Place	Date Nov	Hour	Summary of Events and Information	Remarks and references to Appendices
Ploegsteert Trenches	28th		The usual relief was carried out without casualties. B D & C Companies posted in the firing trenches A Coy being in support at Lancashire Support Farm. Relief carried out quicker than usual.	
Trenches	29th		Nothing of importance to record. Preliminary measures were discussed with regard to a proposed mining operation opposite the centre trenches at present occupied by D Coy. A quiet day. Less sniping than usual	
	30th		The usual fatigues were carried on during the day. Water again bad in the front line trenches, especially B Coy. A quiet day. During the early hours of the evening the enemy sent up an unusual number of very lights. A patrol from B Coy went out to see condition of enemy's wire near the new work which they are constructing. Machine guns on both sides were unusually active about 10.30 pm on our right.	

$353 Wt. W2544/1454 700,000 5/15 D. D. & L. A.D.S.S./Forms/C. 2118.

25th Div

8th Border Regt:

Vol: 3

121 / 7935

nil
[illegible]

Army Form C. 2118.

Instructions regarding War Diaries and Intelligence Summaries are contained in F. S. Regs., Part II. and the Staff Manual respectively. Title pages will be prepared in manuscript.

WAR DIARY
or
INTELLIGENCE SUMMARY.

(*Erase heading not required.*)

Place	Date Dec	Hour	Summary of Events and Information	Remarks and references to Appendices
Trenches	1st		A quiet day, very little sniping. Had warning that the artillery would be firing on enemy's trenches near Birdcage. A Company sent 3 platoons into the front line trenches keeping one platoon in support at Lancashire Support Farm. These platoons were recalled at the evening stand to.	
	2nd		The morning was quiet. Sniping continued all day. Pte Edwards of B Coy was badly wounded about 2pm. Great difficulty is being experienced with the water in the trenches the left of B Coy being particularly bad. About 7pm the enemy exploded a mine in trench 99 belonging to the 9th L. Lancs. Heavy firing on both sides was the result of this. Lt Gray took a party of 12 men over to trench No 99 to help to repair parapet and search for missing men.	
Trenches & Ploegsteert	3rd		The usual relief took place in the afternoon without any casualties. A very wet day. Great delay in obtaining the Battn baggage on account of new regulations with regard to the transport. Very little sniping.	
	4th		A quiet day. The Battn went to the baths and spent remainder of day in their billets cleaning up and resting. Hyde Farm was shelled by the enemy but luckily no casualties.	

2353 Wt. W2544/1454 700,000 5/15 D. D. & L. A.D.S.S./Forms/C. 2118.

Instructions regarding War Diaries and Intelligence Summaries are contained in F. S. Regs., Part II. and the Staff Manual respectively. Title pages will be prepared in manuscript.

WAR DIARY
or
INTELLIGENCE SUMMARY.
(Erase heading not required.)

Army Form C. 2118.

Place	Date Dec	Hour	Summary of Events and Information	Remarks and references to Appendices
Ploegsteert	5th		The usual fatigues were told off. These were withdrawn at 1 o'clock. Some shell fire was fired at all the billets during the afternoon. About 12.30 this H.E. shell burst over Soyer Farm where A Coy is billeted. There were two casualties Sgt Robinson badly wounded also Pte Walthew slightly wounded. Otherwise quiet day.	
	6th		A Coy erected wire entanglements for the purpose of experiment with reference to their projected night operation. Soyer Farm was shelled during the morning but no casualties. The remaining companies did the usual fatigue. The wire cutters of the Coy was blown off by the R.E. Result, the trip wire blown in half. The charge being a 3lbs.	
	7th		The experiment with the blowing up of the wire entanglements was again tried with better results. Wire being used, the company demolished it. A quiet day.	
Ploegsteert & Trenches	8th		The usual relief took place. The 2nd S Lancs taking our place in billets. D A & C Companies in firing line. B Coy in Lancashire Support Farm. More firing than usual took place during the evening and at midnight.	
	9th		During the morning a 9.2 howitzer at [illegible] Farm bombarded the German fort opposite trench 110 doing considerable damage. Unfortunately one shell burst short and blew up D Coy	

Army Form C. 2118.

Instructions regarding War Diaries and Intelligence Summaries are contained in F. S. Regs., Part II. and the Staff Manual respectively. Title pages will be prepared in manuscript.

WAR DIARY
or
INTELLIGENCE SUMMARY.

(Erase heading not required.)

Place	Date Dec	Hour	Summary of Events and Information	Remarks and references to Appendices
Trenches	9th		headquarters no one was near the spot at the time. During the night the R. Warnow rose considerably and the front trench about 30 yards either side became badly flooded. The enemy dropped about 30 shells N & E of Lancashire Support Farm but did no damage	
Trenches	10th		During the night the water again rose. A Coy especially had great difficulty in coping with it and had to abandon about 8 bays South of 101/2. The day was calm.	
	11th		Water in the trenches had subsided about 8 inches. The parapets were repaired as much of them had subsided. About 2 pm the enemy again shelled the vicinity of Lancashire Support Farm and the tram line, no damage was done.	
	12th		The 9th Loyal N Lancs took over Fort Paul & Fort Hadley. "C" Coy extended their line northwards to the R. Warnow. "A" Coy on account of flooded dugouts had to send 1 Platoon to billet with B Coy at Lancashire Support Farm and 1 Platoon from B Coy came to Mountain Gun Farm for billets. During the afternoon considerable shelling took place. In the morning 2Lt Carruthers ~~[illegible]~~ C Coy was seriously wounded in the head. The water in 105 & 106 subsided a little during the day.	
Trench line Ploegsteert	13		Relieved by the 2nd S. Lancs during the afternoon. The Batt returned to their usual billets.	

2353 Wt. W2544/1454 700,000 5/15 D. D. & L. A.D.S.S./Forms/C. 2118.

Instructions regarding War Diaries and Intelligence Summaries are contained in F. S. Regs., Part II. and the Staff Manual respectively. Title pages will be prepared in manuscript.

WAR DIARY
or
INTELLIGENCE SUMMARY.
(Erase heading not required.)

Army Form C. 2118.

Place	Date	Hour	Summary of Events and Information	Remarks and references to Appendices
Ploegsteert	14th		The Battn rested in billets and during the day went by Companies to Pont de Nieppe for baths. D Coy supplied night fatigue. Cpl [illegible] Hill [illegible] wounded by splinter of shell.	
	15th		A B and C Companies furnished fatigue for the Engineers at Touquet Berthe also night carrying parties from Touquet Berthe to Lancashire Support Farm	
	16th		The usual shelling of Ploegsteert village took place. The Brigade H Q had a few shells close to them also B Coy at [illegible] Farm. The [illegible] school had two shells [illegible] of the [illegible] attending the school were killed. The usual fatigues were carried out	
	17th		A very quiet day, the usual fatigues were found. A Coy supplied 1 NCO and 20 men for a night fatigue at Touquet Berthe	
Ploegsteert & Trenches	18th		The usual relief was carried out. The relief started at 2 pm. D Coy occupied the right sector A the centre and B Coy on the left. C Coy in Lancashire Support Farm. Col Brander took over the command of the 7th Inf Bde	
	19th		Lt Col C J Bond took over command of the Regt from Col Brander who proceeded home. A quiet day very little sniping. All companies were employed in repairing parapets. A Coy supplied a	

2353 Wt. W2544/1454 700,000 5/15 D. D. & L. A.D.S.S./Forms/C. 2118.

Army Form C. 2118.

Instructions regarding War Diaries and Intelligence Summaries are contained in F. S. Regs., Part II. and the Staff Manual respectively. Title pages will be prepared in manuscript.

WAR DIARY
or
INTELLIGENCE SUMMARY.
(Erase heading not required.)

Place	Date Dec	Hour	Summary of Events and Information	Remarks and references to Appendices
			Fatigue party for bringing up stores from Touquet Berthe	
Trenches	20th		Each company employed in repairing their parapet and freeing trenches from water. L/Corp Smith of D Coy was killed while working in C T 101/3. OC 8th S Lancashire Regt visited the line with a view to taking over when relief takes place. At 2pm a bombardment of the enemy's front line trench by trench Mortars took place. The Germans retaliated. There were no casualties.	
	21st		A quiet day, very wet. The officers commanding Companies of the 8th S Lanc Regt went round the trenches during the morning, with a view to taking over the line	
	22nd		All available men were employed in repairing parapets, and improving communication trenches. A Coy started new dug out on the western side of the road in rear of their support line. Quiet day, the right Coy was shelled about 11am, about 7 shells falling in that area	
Trenches & Ploegsteert	23rd		The Battalion was relieved by the 8th S Lancs Regt during the afternoon. There were no casualties	
Ploegsteert	24th		The Battalion rested in billets and had baths at Nieppe during the day. A night fatigue party was supplied both by B & D Companies	
	25th		Service was held at Hyde Farm nearly 250 men present. There were fewer fatigues. A Coy supplied 30 men during the afternoon. Quiet day.	

Instructions regarding War Diaries and Intelligence Summaries are contained in F. S. Regs., Part II. and the Staff Manual respectively. Title pages will be prepared in manuscript.

WAR DIARY
or
INTELLIGENCE SUMMARY.
(Erase heading not required.)

Army Form C. 2118.

Place	Date	Hour	Summary of Events and Information	Remarks and references to Appendices
Ploegsteert	26th		Ploegsteert was shelled during the morning and evening. All the Companies were on fatigue work during the morning. In the evening A B & C Companies supplied fatigue parties for the R.E.	
Ploegsteert & Trenches	27th		The Battalion went into the trenches at 6.30 am relieving the 8th S Lancs Regt. The [?] Cheshires were on our left and L N Lancs on our right. C Coy were the right of our line A Coy Centre and B Coy on left.	
	28th		All companies were employed in repairing & remaking parapets and draining trenches. At 9.10 pm a mine operation was [illegible] of the Batt on our right. There was a good deal of rifle fire and a bombardment lasting for about an hour. B Coy had one man [illegible]. Casualties [illegible]	
	29th		Nothing of importance occurred during the day	
	30th		The enemy's snipers were most active this [?] Pte Ellis Jones of B Coy was killed in C.T. 102. The Batt was engaged in repairing the parapets & draining trenches	
	31st		A quiet day. At midnight 10 rounds rapid were fired in reply to German fusilade. There were no casualties.	

2353 Wt. W2544/1454 700,000 5/15 D. D. & L. A.D.S.S./Forms/C. 2118.

75th Inf. Bde.

25th Division

8th Battn.

BORDER REGIMENT,

JANUARY, 1916.

H. N.
7 sheets

8th Border Rgt:
Vol: 4
JULY 1916

25

Instructions regarding War Diaries and Intelligence Summaries are contained in F. S. Regs., Part II. and the Staff Manual respectively. Title pages will be prepared in manuscript.

WAR DIARY
or
INTELLIGENCE SUMMARY.
(*Erase heading not required.*)

Army Form C. 2118.

Place	Date Jan 1916	Hour	Summary of Events and Information	Remarks and references to Appendices
Trenches	1st		The expected retaliation to our fusilade last night did not materialize. On the whole a quiet day. Sniping was more active on both sides.	
Trenches & Ploegsteert	2nd		Relieved by the 2nd Battn S. Lancs Regt during the afternoon, the relief took place later than usual owing to the clear weather. There were no casualties.	
	3rd		The Battalion rested in billets. At 6 pm a fatigue party of 1 Officer and 80 men were told off to assist the R.E. 250 men were sent to the Bath.	
	4th		A. B. & C Companies supplied the usual fatigues.	
	5th		Nothing of importance to relate	
	6th		A quiet day. The enemy shelled the Northern end of Ploegsteert but did little damage a few shells fell near Battn H.Q	
Ploegsteert Trenches	7th		The usual relief took place at 3.30 pm there were no casualties. On account of the recent shelling of Battn H.Q the Machine Gun Section was billeted in Lancashire Support Farm. The XI Cheshire Regt is on our left & the Lancs Fusiliers on our right. A Coy in Lanc Support Farm	
	8th		The enemy were particularly active with regard to sniping especially at "Stand to" in the evening, there were no casualties. The repairing of the parapet & building parados occupied the Companies during the day. At 8 pm fatigue party from A Coy	

#353 Wt. W2544/1454 700,000 5/15 D. D. & L. A.D.S.S./Forms/C. 2118.

Instructions regarding War Diaries and Intelligence Summaries are contained in F. S. Regs., Part II. and the Staff Manual respectively. Title pages will be prepared in manuscript.

WAR DIARY
or
INTELLIGENCE SUMMARY.
(Erase heading not required.)

Army Form C. 2118.

Place	Date	Hour	Summary of Events and Information	Remarks and references to Appendices
[illegible] Trenches	9th		The enemy shelled our sector more than usual. Lancashire Support Farm had a few Shrapnel bursts within 100 yards. Sniping not so active as yesterday. A Coy supplied night working parties also carrying parties	
[illegible] "	10th		Laurence Farm considerably shelled during the morning. 18 H.E. falling within a few yards of the Farm. The tram line was cut in two places but repaired by the R.E. One man Pte [illegible] of A Coy slightly wounded in the back. No damage was done	
[illegible] "	11th		The enemy again shelled Laurence Farm. 8 H.E. shells were fired. There were no casualties or any damage done	
[illegible] "	12th		A quiet day with the exception of the afternoon when from 4 pm – 4.30 pm the Germans fired 25 shells which fell in the vicinity of Lancashire Support Farm and Laurence Farm. There was no damage. The usual work was carried on in the front line trenches.	
[illegible] Trenches & Ploegsteert	13th		The usual relief took place. We were relieved by the 2nd S Lancs Regt. On account of the German shelling the relief took place after 4.30 pm.	
	14th		The [illegible] with the exception of A Coy were employed on various fatigues	

2353 Wt. W2544/1454 700,000 5/15 D. D. & L. A.D.S.S./Forms/C. 2118.

Instructions regarding War Diaries and Intelligence Summaries are contained in F. S. Regs., Part II. and the Staff Manual respectively. Title pages will be prepared in manuscript.

WAR DIARY
or
INTELLIGENCE SUMMARY.
(Erase heading not required.)

Army Form C. 2118.

Place	Date	Hour	Summary of Events and Information	Remarks and references to Appendices
Ploegsteert	15th		Ploegsteert received about 15 H E Shell during the afternoon. The Soldiers Home was demolished but apart from this little damage was done.	
"	16th		Divine Service was held at Soyer Farm at 9.31 am. Quiet day	
"	17th		Nothing of importance to relate. A lecture was held at Bailleul. 9 officers attended. Ploegsteert had a few shells about 6 pm and again at 8.15 pm	
"	18th		The usual fatigues were furnished. Exceptionally quiet day. Wet	
" in trenches	19th		The usual relief took place before daybreak. C Coy on right. A Coy in centre and D Coy on left. B Coy in reserve. Just after the relief 2Lt Gray was slightly wounded in the eye. The Germans put a few shells near Lancashire Support Farm about 10.30 am and also shelled the main communication trench. At 12.30 pm a minor operation started on our right. This was carried out by the 74th Bde. The Battn supported their attack at 4.30 by rifle fire, machine guns, and grenades. The Germans replied by shelling our line. We had 6 casualties, all of A Coy. Pte Fitzwilliams & Pte Tyson both seriously wounded L/C Williamson & L/C J Thornton slightly wounded Pte Coates & Woodhead slightly wounded & Pte McGann B Coy also slightly wounded.	
"	20th		A quiet day. Col Winston Churchill inspected our lines with a view to taking them over. During the night Lt Warren & Cpl Hodgson went on patrol. They did not return, no evidence is forthcoming as to what happened to them.	

Instructions regarding War Diaries and Intelligence Summaries are contained in F. S. Regs., Part II. and the Staff Manual respectively. Title pages will be prepared in manuscript.

WAR DIARY
or
INTELLIGENCE SUMMARY.

(*Erase heading not required.*)

Army Form C. 2118.

Place	Date	Hour	Summary of Events and Information	Remarks and references to Appendices
Trenches	Jan 21st		The Coy Commanders of the relieving Battn inspected our trenches during the morning. There was considerably more sniping than usual during the late hours of the afternoon and the evening.	
	22nd		A quiet day nothing of importance to record. The usual work on drains and parapets etc was carried out	
Trenches & Ploegsteert	23rd		The Battn relieved by the 2nd S Lancs. The relief commenced at 5 pm and was finished by 7 pm. There were no casualties. There was not more sniping than usual during the relief.	
Ploegsteert	24		Nothing of importance done except a few fatigues. Coys arranging for move back on 26th.	
—do—	25.		Everything packed up for move tomorrow. A Coy borrowed cart from the farm which took Coys blankets. 2 Motor lorries arrived for greatcoats & blankets.	
—do—	26		Battalion moved out from Ploegsteert and marched to Billets at LA CRECHE. Start was made at 5 a.m. 20 minutes being allowed between Coys to pass X roads at Church. Arrived at La Creche about 8 a.m. Advance party of 1 officer & 8 O.R took over billets night before. Stayed at this place for one day only.	

2353 Wt. W2544/1454/ 700,000 5/15 D. D. & L. A.D.S.S./Forms/C. 2118.

Instructions regarding War Diaries and Intelligence Summaries are contained in F. S. Regs., Part II. and the Staff Manual respectively. Title pages will be prepared in manuscript.

Army Form C. 2118.

WAR DIARY
or
INTELLIGENCE SUMMARY.
(Erase heading not required.)

Place	Date	Hour	Summary of Events and Information	Remarks and references to Appendices
La Creche.	27.		Moved off at 6 a.m to Strazeele. Arrived about 10 a.m after a good march, few men falling out. Billets at Strazeele were again taken over by ~~advan~~ advance party of same strength as before. Coys rather far apart but billets good on the whole. Took over from the 6th Scottish Rifles (Cameronians). Billets untidy & in a bad state.	
Strazeele	28		Cleaning up, no work done as other Battalions had not arrived from Ploegsteert yet. Day quiet, nothing to report.	
– do –	29		D Coy changed Billets as they were so far away from others. Got much better Billet nearer other Coys.	
– do –	30		Other Battalions arrived in Strazeele. Rearguard joined up here again and reported all handing over done correctly.	
– do –	31		Coys went on Route march from their different billets of about 4 miles length. Games &c being played in afternoon.	

C. E. Bond Lt Col.
Comdg [illegible]

2353 Wt. W2544/1454 700,000 5/15 D. D. & L. A.D.S.S./Forms/C. 2118.

75th Inf. Bde.

25th Division

8th Battn.

BORDER REGIMENT,

F E B R U A R Y, 1 9 1 6.

8th Baden Reg

25th Div

Vol 5.

75 Bde

5 N.
2 sheets

Army Form C. 2118.

Instructions regarding War Diaries and Intelligence Summaries are contained in F. S. Regs., Part II. and the Staff Manual respectively. Title pages will be prepared in manuscript.

WAR DIARY
or
INTELLIGENCE SUMMARY.
(Erase heading not required.)

Place	Date	Hour	Summary of Events and Information	Remarks and references to Appendices
Strazeele	1/2/16		All Coys. in Billets and settled down. Companies doing training under Coy arrangements.	
	2-2-16		6 Officers went to Lecture at Bailleul Subject Preliminary Bombardment by Major McLean. Coys went for a short Route March.	
	3/2/16		Lecture in Bailleul by Capt Lee J. Keane on Trench Mortar Organization and employment.	
	4/2/16		Company training	
	5/2/16		Company training afternoon devoted to field sports	
	6/2/16		Church parade at Transport lines	
	7/2/16		Company training & route march	
	8/2/16		Genl Woodward relinquished command of the Brigade	
	9/2/16		The Brigade inspected on route march by Genl Plumer during the morning	
	10/2/16		The Brigade inspected on route march by Lord Kitchener.	

E. E. Hoult Lt Col
Comdg 8th Border Regt

8353 Wt. W2544/1454 700,000 5/15 D. D. & L. A.D.S.S./Forms/C. 2118.

Army Form C. 2118.

Instructions regarding War Diaries and Intelligence Summaries are contained in F. S. Regs., Part II. and the Staff Manual respectively. Title pages will be prepared in manuscript.

WAR DIARY
or
INTELLIGENCE SUMMARY.

(Erase heading not required.)

Place	Date Feb	Hour	Summary of Events and Information	Remarks and references to Appendices
Strazeele	11th		Company training.	
	12th		Company training. Football during the afternoon.	
	13th		Church parade during the morning held in field near B Coy.	
	14th		Battalion engaged in training.	
	15th		Usual training during the morning. In the afternoon cross country race open to all units of the Division. Won by Border Horse 8th Border 2nd.	
	16th		Special training in use of gas helmet.	
	17th 18th		Company & Battalion training. Lecture by Capt Fitzpatrick on "Engineering work in the Field".	
	19		Brigade Sports.	
	20th		Church parade in morning. Brigade cross country race was held in the afternoon won by A Coy 8th Borders. Gold medal won by Cpl Close.	

C. E. Bond Lt Col.
Comdg. 8th Border Regt.

2353 Wt. W2544/1454 700,000 5/15 D. D. & L. A.D.S.S./Forms/C. 2118.

Army Form C. 2118.

Instructions regarding War Diaries and Intelligence Summaries are contained in F. S. Regs., Part II. and the Staff Manual respectively. Title pages will be prepared in manuscript.

WAR DIARY
or
INTELLIGENCE SUMMARY.
(Erase heading not required.)

Place	Date	Hour	Summary of Events and Information	Remarks and references to Appendices
Strazeele.	21st		Company training and machine gun training for all companies.	
	22nd 23rd 24th		Company training including bayonet fighting, physical drill, route marching and gas helmet drill.	
	25th		16 officers & 132 men proceeded to Outtersteene to see demonstration of German Flammenwerfer. In evening concert given by 8th Border Regt.	
	26th		Training considerably hindered on account of snow. Brigade boxing competition in evening. Lecture at 4pm by Col Richardson on "Sniping".	
	28th		Company training and route march.	
	27th		Church parade.	
	29th		Brigade night march.	

C. L. Bond Lt Col
Comdg 8th Border Regt

75th Inf. Bde.

25th Division.

8th Battn.

BORDER REGIMENT,

M A R C H, 1 9 1 6.

Instructions regarding War Diaries and Intelligence Summaries are contained in F. S. Regs., Part II. and the Staff Manual respectively. Title pages will be prepared in manuscript.

Army Form C. 2118.

WAR DIARY
or
INTELLIGENCE SUMMARY.
(Erase heading not required.)

Place	Date	Hour	Summary of Events and Information	Remarks and references to Appendices
Strazeele	1st		Route march full companies.	
	2nd		A & B Companies route march C & D Companies field training and bayonet fighting.	
	3rd–7th		Company & Battalion training	
	8th		Brigade route march 12 miles.	
	9th		Battalion employed in handing in stores, cleaning billets etc.	
Strazeele & Boeseghem	10th		The Battalion left Strazeele and marched to Boeseghem via Hazebrouck and billeted there for the night	
Boeseghem Nedon	11th		The Battalion left Boeseghem and marched to Nedon to billets	

P. Sheehan Major
Comdg. 8th Border Regiment

£353 Wt. W2544/1454 700,000 5/15 D. D. & L. A.D.S.S./Forms/C. 2118.

Army Form C. 2118.

Instructions regarding War Diaries and Intelligence Summaries are contained in F. S. Regs., Part II. and the Staff Manual respectively. Title pages will be prepared in manuscript.

WAR DIARY
or
INTELLIGENCE SUMMARY.

(Erase heading not required.)

Place	Date March	Hour	Summary of Events and Information	Remarks and references to Appendices
Rieux	12th		In billets resting.	
	13th		All companies practised in the attack of open warfare during the morning.	
	14th		The Battalion was inspected in the attack by the Brigadier	
	15th		All companies practised in open order drill	
Rieux Bryas	16th		The Battalion left Rieux and marched to Bryas arriving at 1 pm.	
	17th		Company Inspections etc	
	18th		Route march by Companies 8 miles. C Coy marched to St Pol & billeted there	
	19th		Church parade and Inspection.	
	20th		The Battalion was inspected by Sir Julian Byng in the grounds of the Chateau de Bryas and marched past in column of route.	
	21st		Brigade practised in the attack. The xi Cheshires detailed as defending force. The attack carried out by 2nd S Lancs Regt on the Right, 8th Border Regt in the centre, 8th S Lancs Regt on the left.	
	22nd		Companies went a route march	
	23rd		The Commanding Officer, 2nd in command, adjutant & signalling officer visited the Southern portion of the new sector of the line of trenches, only the subsidiary line was visited.	

[signature] Major
Comdg. 8th Border Regt

Army Form C. 2118.

Instructions regarding War Diaries and Intelligence Summaries are contained in F. S. Regs., Part II. and the Staff Manual respectively. Title pages will be prepared in manuscript.

WAR DIARY
or
INTELLIGENCE SUMMARY.
(Erase heading not required.)

Place	Date	Hour	Summary of Events and Information	Remarks and references to Appendices
	March			
Bryas.	24th		On account of the bad weather a Brigade concentration march was postponed. The companies were inspected under Coy arrangements and lectures given.	
	25th		The northern sector of the new line of trenches was visited, only the subsidiary line was seen.	
	26th		Church Parades and inspections	
	27th		Brigade concentration march	
	28th		Battalion training. Attack & advanced guard.	
	29th		The Battalion was practiced in night outposts north of Bryas.	
	30th		Route March	
	31st		The Battalion moved to MONCHY BRETON and was inspected by the C. in C near MARQUAY while on the march	

P. [illegible] Major
Comdg. 8th Border Regt.

8353 Wt. W2544/1454 700,000 5/15 D. D. & L. A.D.S.S./Forms/C. 2118.

75th Inf. Bde.

25th Division

8th Battn.

BORDER REGIMENT,

A P R I L, 1 9 1 6.

(for entries 27th - 30th April,
see May Diary)

APRIL + ~~MAY~~

XXV

Instructions regarding War Diaries and Intelligence Summaries are contained in F. S. Regs., Part II. and the Staff Manual respectively. Title pages will be prepared in manuscript.

WAR DIARY
or
INTELLIGENCE SUMMARY.

(Erase heading not required.)

8TH (SERVICE) BATTALION, THE BORDER REGIMENT.

Army Form C. 2118.

Vol. 7+8

Place	Date	Hour	Summary of Events and Information	Remarks and references to Appendices
MONCHY BRETON	April 1		The Battalion was inspected at close order drill by the Corps Commander in the morning. Companies cleaned billets during the afternoon	
	2nd		Church parade	
	3rd		The Battalion was engaged in wood fighting, attack & defence	
	4th		Route March	
	5th		Company drill in the morning. Brigade concentration night march and attack of a position	
	6th		Company training communication drill for N.C.Os	
	7th		Battalion practised in attack on trenches	
	8th		C Coy at ST POL relieved by D Coy. 100 men of B Coy on fatigue at bombing school. A Coy at range in morning.	
	9th		Church Parades.	
	10th		Bn practised as Advance Guard to Inf. Bde in Hostile country. Communication Drill for NCOs. Col. Bond to Div School.	7.N. 9th

8353 Wt. W2544/1454 700,000 5/15 D. D. & L. A.D.S.S./Forms/C. 2118.

Instructions regarding War Diaries and Intelligence Summaries are contained in F. S. Regs., Part II. and the Staff Manual respectively. Title pages will be prepared in manuscript.

WAR DIARY
or
INTELLIGENCE SUMMARY.

(Erase heading not required.)

Army Form C. 2118.

8TH (SERVICE) BATTALION,
THE BORDER REGIMENT.

Place	Date	Hour	Summary of Events and Information	Remarks and references to Appendices
Morchy Breton	Apl. 11		Very wet. Companies exercised in Musketry & Close Order. Billets cleaned up. Lecture to NCOs & Officers. D	
	12		Very wet. Companies exercised in Musketry & Close order. 250 men to demonstration of Flame projector. D	
	13		Showery. Companies exercised in Musketry, & close order. Squads practised in firing Lewis Gun on miniature range. Lecture to Officers & NCOs. D	
	14		Brigade Concentration March & inspection by Corps Commander. Communication Drill for NCOs. afternoon Lewis Gun firing on range. D	
	15		Companies exercised in Close Order Drill & Musketry & Bayonet fighting. Lewis Gun firing on range. C.O. went up to inspect front line trenches occupied by 46th Division.	
	16		Church parades & Kit inspections. D	
	17		The C.O Adjutant and Company Commanders visited the new front line trenches north of Arras.	
	18th		Company Commanders proceeded to Dommville to see demonstration of Flammenwerfer.	
	19th		Company parades and training.	

8353 Wt. W2544/1454 700,000 5/15 D. D. & L. A.D.S.S./Forms/C. 2118.

Instructions regarding War Diaries and Intelligence Summaries are contained in F. S. Regs., Part II. and the Staff Manual respectively. Title pages will be prepared in manuscript.

WAR DIARY
or
INTELLIGENCE SUMMARY.
(Erase heading not required.)

8TH (SERVICE) BATTALION, THE BORDER REGIMENT.

Army Form C. 2118.

Place	Date	Hour	Summary of Events and Information	Remarks and references to Appendices
Monchy Breton	April 20th		The Battalion was employed in cleaning up billets and preparing to hand over to the incoming unit (1/6 S Stafford Regt).	
[illegible] Bertonval Trenches	21st		The Battalion proceeded to Ecoivres at 2.30 pm in Motor Lorries and busses halted there till 7.30 pm and then proceeded to relieve the 1/6 S Stafford Regt in the trenches north of Neuville St Vaast. We connected up with the 1st Wiltshire Regt of the 7th Bde on our left and with 2nd Battn S Lancashire Regt on our right. D C & A Companies in the firing line B Coy in reserve.	
Trenches	22		The relief completed at 4-31 am. Repairs of trenches much hindered by	
	22		Continuous rain	
	23rd		The Battalion was employed in repairing and improving trenches.	
	24th		The Battalion was employed in draining trenches of water and taking up boards and relaying, also repairing trenches.	
	25th 26		As on 23rd & 24th. On the 25th at 11.15 pm our advanced posts were bombed & again at 8 am on the 26th unfortunately we had casualties one sergeant killed and 5 men wounded two seriously.	

2353 Wt. W2544/1454 700,000 5/15 D. D. & L. A.D.S.S./Forms/C. 2118.

75th Inf. Bde.

25th Division.

8th Battn.

BORDER REGIMENT,

M A Y, 1 9 1 6.

Instructions regarding War Diaries and Intelligence Summaries are contained in F. S. Regs., Part II. and the Staff Manual respectively. Title pages will be prepared in manuscript.

WAR DIARY
or
INTELLIGENCE SUMMARY.
(Erase heading not required.)

Army Form C. 2118.

8TH (SERVICE) BATTALION, THE BORDER REGIMENT.

27/4 – 31/5/16

Place	Date	Hour	Summary of Events and Information	Remarks and references to Appendices
Trenches	April 27th		The Battalion was relieved during the night by the XI Cheshire Regt	
	28th		The Battalion rested in Senlis [illegible] and were engaged in cleaning up Equipment clothing etc. During the afternoon C & D Coys furnished working parties in the support line. At 7.30 pm while D Coy were working a shell burst in the middle of one section killing 1 Sergeant 2 men and injuring 6 others. Later one of the wounded men died. Stand to alarm from 9 pm – 11.30 pm	
	29th		The Battalion furnished fatigues for the construction of new support line and the repair of existing Communication trenches	
	30th		The Battalion provided working parties for construction of Sunken line & General repair of Communication Trenches	P Shaw Maj 8th Border Regt
	May 1st		During the day & night the Battalion provided necessary working & carrying parties for construction of Sunken Line & repair of C.Ts.	
	2nd		Col Bond returned to Battalion from the Divisional School at Buneville. The Battalion provided necessary fatigue parties for repairing CTs & building the Sunken Line.	
	3rd		During the day the Battalion provided fatigue parties as before, and in the evening relieved the XIth Cheshire Regiment in the trenches of the left Sector of the Brigade front – A B & D in firing line & C Coy in Reserve. D Coy had little Bombing on their Y Post. Bombing accident in D Coy lines	

2353 Wt. W2544/1454 700,000 5/15 D. D. & L. A.D.S.S./Forms/C. 2118.

Instructions regarding War Diaries and Intelligence Summaries are contained in F. S. Regs., Part II. and the Staff Manual respectively. Title pages will be prepared in manuscript.

WAR DIARY
or
INTELLIGENCE SUMMARY.
(Erase heading not required.)

Army Form C. 2118.

8TH (SERVICE) BATTALION, THE BORDER REGIMENT.

Place	Date May	Hour	Summary of Events and Information	Remarks and references to Appendices
TRENCHES	4.		Battalion in trenches. A start was made on the new Doublement line behind the front line. General repair & upkeep of trenches also engaged attention.	
	5.	3 am	Enemy put up 3 mines simultaneously, 1 opposite ~~left~~ right of 064 & 2 in front of 063. They had the effect of extending the old craters (063.1 & 064.1) & much of our lip subsided. No enemy attack was made, nor were any of our works damaged. We suffered no casualties. There was no Artillery fire. Rifles & Machine Guns together with Bombs being employed where necessary. During the day the Battalion was employed on general repair work & in strengthening & consolidating our forward posts. The new Doublement line was progressed with during the night.	
	6.		Nothing of importance occurred except in Y Post where there was an occasional bombing duel. The old De la Fosse trench leading from Crater 063/1 was opened up as far as Doublement, which latter trench was also progressed with during the night. Wiring the intervals of trench 063 was begun.	
	7.		The day was quiet with a little bombing at night, especially in Y Post. Work on the Soutien was proceeded with & the Doublement was extended behind 065.	
	8.		In retaliation for some Medium Mortar bombs & Stokes mortar bombs which we put over, the enemy crumped the Soutien line. No damage was done. Towards evening, by means of bombs & Rifle Grenades B Coy blew in an enemy post on the eastern lip of crater 064/2.	
	9.		The day passed quietly except towards evening, when there was considerable Artillery activity. For blowing in this post yesterday the enemy retaliated by bombing our Y Post. ~~[illegible] Y Post [illegible]~~	

8353 Wt. W2544/1454 700,000 5/15 D. D. & L. A.D.S.S./Forms/C. 2118.

Instructions regarding War Diaries and Intelligence Summaries are contained in F. S. Regs., Part II. and the Staff Manual respectively. Title pages will be prepared in manuscript.

WAR DIARY
or
INTELLIGENCE SUMMARY.
(Erase heading not required.)

8TH (SERVICE) BATTALION, THE BORDER REGIMENT.

Army Form C. 2118.

Place	Date May	Hour	Summary of Events and Information	Remarks and references to Appendices
TRENCHES	9 (cont)		We had one casualty. The Battalion was relieved by the XI Cheshire Regt at night & reached the huts in ECOIVRE without incident.	
Ecoivres	10th–15th		In billets.	
	16th		The Battalion went into 1st line trenches relieving the XI Cheshires. The 2nd S. Lancs on our right and the 1st Wilts on our left.	
	17th		The usual repairs and improvements were made. Quiet day.	
	18th		Considerable shelling by the enemy also they were throwing our more bombs & grenades than usual. We had 2 killed and 12 wounded.	
	19th		The enemy again active. We had 1 man wounded & Lt Hickomon wounded.	

£353 Wt. W2544/1454 700,000 5/15 D. D. & L. A.D.S.S./Forms/C. 2118.

Instructions regarding War Diaries and Intelligence Summaries are contained in F. S. Regs., Part II. and the Staff Manual respectively. Title pages will be prepared in manuscript.

WAR DIARY
or
INTELLIGENCE SUMMARY.
(*Erase heading not required.*)

Army Form C. 2118.

8TH (SERVICE) BATTALION, THE BORDER REGIMENT.

Place	Date May	Hour	Summary of Events and Information	Remarks and references to Appendices
Trenches	20th		The Battalion went into Brigade Reserve at Neuville St Vaast being relieved by the 11th Cheshires. The relief was carried out during the afternoon. No casualties.	
Neuville St Vaast	21st		The enemy shelled the village intermittently throughout the day and dropped "Tear Shells" these being the first the Battalion has experienced. No casualties. The usual fatigues were furnished.	
	22nd		The enemy again shelled the village with Tear Shells otherwise the day was quiet.	
	23rd		About 20 large shells were fired into the village, no damage was done & no casualties.	
	24th		The Battalion relieved the 11th Cheshires in the front line trenches. 2nd Batt S. Lancs on our right 1st Batt Wiltshires on our left.	
	25th		The enemy shelled our front line & support trenches during the morning. We had two men wounded.	

\#353 Wt. W2544/1454 700,000 5/15 D. D. & L. A.D.S.S./Forms/C. 2118.

Instructions regarding War Diaries and Intelligence Summaries are contained in F. S. Regs., Part II. and the Staff Manual respectively. Title pages will be prepared in manuscript.

WAR DIARY
or
INTELLIGENCE SUMMARY.
(Erase heading not required.)

8TH (SERVICE) BATTALION, THE BORDER REGIMENT.

Army Form C. 2118.

Place	Date	Hour	Summary of Events and Information	Remarks and references to Appendices
	May			
Trenches	26th		The usual shelling took place, but little damage done. 2/Lieuts Adams & Bowen both slightly wounded by a bomb, also two privates.	
	27th		A quiet day no casualties.	
	28th		Our front line & support line trenches were subjected to artillery fire and mortars for the greater part of the day. Our casualties were 1 man of A Coy wounded, 6 wounded & 2 killed in B Coy and 1 wounded in D Coy.	
	29th		A fairly quiet day the Battalion was employed in opening up & strengthening new trenches especially on our left. We had two men of B Coy slightly wounded by a bomb.	
	30th		The enemy blew a mine in front of our centre Coy (B) a platoon was sent forward and immediately occupied & consolidated the near lip of the crater. The only casualty was a man of A who died later. No damage was done.	

2353 Wt. W2544/1454 700,000 5/15 D. D. & L. A.D.S.S./Forms/C. 2118.

Army Form C. 2118.

Instructions regarding War Diaries and Intelligence Summaries are contained in F. S. Regs., Part II. and the Staff Manual respectively. Title pages will be prepared in manuscript.

WAR DIARY
or
INTELLIGENCE SUMMARY.
(Erase heading not required.)

8TH (SERVICE) BATTALION, THE BORDER REGIMENT.

Place	Date	Hour	Summary of Events and Information	Remarks and references to Appendices
Trench	May 31st 31		A quiet day on the whole. We had one man L/Cpl Wright of B Coy slightly wounded. We were relieved during the night by the 1/5 Seaforth Highlanders. The Battalion marched to H.Q where they went into billets till the following day.	

J. Shakal Maj
8th Batt Border Regt

2353 Wt. W2544/1454 700,000 5/15 D. D. & L. A.D.S.S./Forms/C. 2118.

75th Inf. Bde.

25th Division

8th Battn.

BORDER REGIMENT,

J U N E, 1 9 1 6.

8TH (SERVICE) BATTALION, THE BORDER REGIMENT.

XXV

Instructions regarding War Diaries and Intelligence Summaries are contained in F. S. Regs., Part II. and the Staff Manual respectively. Title pages will be prepared in manuscript.

75/25

WAR DIARY
or
INTELLIGENCE SUMMARY.
(Erase heading not required.)

8th (Ser) Batt: The Border Regiment

June

THE BORDER REGIMENT. BATTALION.

Army Form C. 2118.

Vol 9

Place	Date 1916	Hour	Summary of Events and Information	Remarks and references to Appendices
ACQ	June 1st		The Battalion remained in billets during the day and at 8.30pm marched to SAVY to billets.	
SAVY	2nd		The Battalion employed in cleaning up. Air baths were allotted to the Companies.	
	3rd		Physical drill and bayonet fighting. Short route march by all Companies.	
	4th		Church Parade during the morning.	
	5th 6th 7th		Battalion employed at [illegible] & [illegible] in Companies training.	
	8th 9th		Battalion training at Musketry [illegible] & [illegible]	
	10th		Brigade field day and training.	

Instructions regarding War Diaries and Intelligence Summaries are contained in F. S. Regs., Part II. and the Staff Manual respectively. Title pages will be prepared in manuscript.

WAR DIARY
or
INTELLIGENCE SUMMARY.
(Erase heading not required.)

8TH (SERVICE) BATTALION, THE BORDER REGIMENT.

Army Form C. 2118.

Place	Date	Hour	Summary of Events and Information	Remarks and references to Appendices
Sary	11th		Church Parade	
	12th		Divisional Field day at Monchy Breton & Chelers	
	13th		Battalion rested in billets. Physical drill & bayonet exercise.	
Bonneville	14th		The Battalion marched at 9-30 am to Bonneville.	
Vacquerie le Boucq	15th		The Battalion marched at 8.30 am to Vacquerie le Boucq arriving about one pm.	
	16th		All Companies were employed in cleaning Equipment etc. Physical exercises and bayonet fighting.	
Bonneville	17th		The Battalion marched at 10-30 pm to Bonneville arriving at 3 am on the 18th. All O.C. Battalions in the Division visited the trenches north of Albert.	
Domart	18th		The Battalion marched at 11.20 pm for Domart arriving there at 2.30 am on the 19th	
	19th		Physical drill & bayonet fighting.	[signature] 8th Border Regt

2353 Wt. W2544/1454 700,000 5/15 D. D. & L. A.D.S.S./Forms/C. 2118.

Instructions regarding War Diaries and Intelligence Summaries are contained in F. S. Regs., Part II. and the Staff Manual respectively. Title pages will be prepared in manuscript.

WAR DIARY
or
INTELLIGENCE SUMMARY.
(Erase heading not required.)

Army Form C. 2118.

8TH (SERVICE) BATTALION, THE BORDER REGIMENT.

Place	Date	Hour	Summary of Events and Information	Remarks and references to Appendices
Dormart	June 20th		Company training and route March	
	21st		Battalion training. Bayonet exercises & Physical exercises	
	22nd		Battalion training	
	23rd		Battalion training & practice for Brigade Cross country race	
	24th		Brigade inter company Cross Country race. Won by A Coy. B Coy second D Coy third.	
Talmas	25th		Regimental Sports. The Battalion marched to Talmas Starting at 9 30 pm arriving at 3 am the 26th	
	26th		Company training and bathing parade	
	27th		Regiment moved to Herissart	
	28th, 29		Regiment remained at Herissart Company training	
	30th		Battalion moved at 9pm to Forceville	

P. STRAHAN.
P Strahan Maj
8th Border Regt

8TH (SERVICE) BATTALION, THE BORDER REGIMENT.

75th Bde.
25th Div.

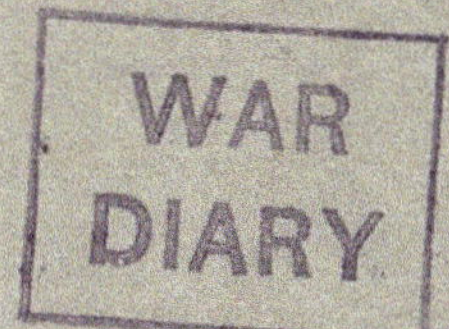

8th BATTALION.

THE BORDER REGIMENT.

JULY 1916

SECRET.

9.N.
9 sheets

To/

The Officer

I/C A. G's Office,

Base.

8 Borders
Vol 10

Herewith War Diary of the Battalion under my Command, for the month of July, 1916.

P. J. Kelly, Maj ....Lieut. Col.,

11th. August, 1916.

Comdg. 8th. Border Regiment.

Instructions regarding War Diaries and Intelligence Summaries are contained in F. S. Regs., Part II. and the Staff Manual respectively. Title pages will be prepared in manuscript.

INTELLIGENCE SUMMARY.

(*Erase heading not required.*)

Place	Date	Hour	Summary of Events and Information	Remarks and references to Appendices
	July			
Franvillers	1st		The Battalion remained halted here for the day, but had sudden orders at 11pm to be ready to move. However the order to move did not come till next day.	
Martinsart Wood	2nd		The Battalion moved to MARTINSART WOOD at 11am. B Team composed of Reserve Officers & N.C.Os moved to VARDENCOURT. The Battn moved to its appointed place in the front line trench South of THIEPVAL preparatory to the attack. The 11 Cheshires on our left and 8th S Lancs Regt on our right. The trenches were heavily shelled by the Germans.	
	3rd		The Regt was supposed to attack the German front line trench at 3am but this was postponed till 6am. The Battalion advanced in 4 waves D & A Coys from our front line B & C Coys from our Support Line, each Company had two Platoons in line covering a front of from 150 to 200 yards followed by the other two platoons. As the leading Companies left the front trench their place was taken by the two leading platoons of each Supporting Company. Touch was kept with the 11 Cheshires	

Instructions regarding War Diaries and Intelligence Summaries are contained in F. S. Regs., Part II. and the Staff Manual respectively. Title pages will be prepared in manuscript.

INTELLIGENCE SUMMARY.

(*Erase heading not required.*)

Place	Date	Hour	Summary of Events and Information	Remarks and references to Appendices
	3rd Continued		by means of runners. This means of communication was also adopted to keep touch with the 2nd S. Lancs Regt. The leading Companies understood their objective and had sufficient time to explain their orders to their men according to the operation orders issued in MARTINSART WOOD. The Coys in support had not sufficient time to explain these orders thoroughly to their men owing to the distance from the front line and the enemy's heavy shell fire. The 1st two Coys went over punctually at the appointed hour, the other two Coys were held in our front line till it was seen how things were going and till reinforcements were required. A message was sent back asking for reinforcements and bombs and these were sent up immediately. 2 platoons at a time were sent up, no reinforcements had arrived from the Reserve to take our place. Eventually all reinforcements were sent except 2 platoons with 2 Lewis guns. The last reserve of 2 platoons did not reach the enemy line but returned with the Battalion when it retired. The frontage occupied in the German line was about 180 yards	

8353 Wt. W2544/1454 700,000 5/15 D. D. & L. A.D.S.S./Forms/C. 2118.

Instructions regarding War Diaries and Intelligence Summaries are contained in F. S. Regs., Part II. and the Staff Manual respectively. Title pages will be prepared in manuscript.

INTELLIGENCE SUMMARY.

(*Erase heading not required.*)

Place	Date	Hour	Summary of Events and Information	Remarks and references to Appendices
	5th Continued		which had been much damaged by our shell fire and there was very little cover. The right flank giving way was the cause of the Battn falling back and also the unfortunate word "retire" was undoubtedly passed along from the right. Major Bird ordered the left to conform. Orders and messages referring to the operations took a very long time to reach Battn H.Q. owing to the dark and the orderlies being new to the trenches. There was no telephone to Battn H.Q. and all messages were by runners, this delayed instructions to O.C. Coys and did not give them time to arrange Bombing parties etc for clearing the German communication trenches. The German rifle & machine gun fire was not particularly severe and had communication with the right & left been kept up throughout the attack would have been successful. During this operation we suffered the following casualties. 4 Officers killed and 10 wounded 430 casualties other ranks [initials]	

8353 Wt. W2544/1454 700,000 5/15 D. D. & L. A.D.S.S./Forms/C. 2118.

Instructions regarding War Diaries and Intelligence Summaries are contained in F. S. Regs., Part II. and the Staff Manual respectively. Title pages will be prepared in manuscript.

INTELLIGENCE SUMMARY.

(*Erase heading not required.*)

Place	Date	Hour	Summary of Events and Information	Remarks and references to Appendices
Martinsart Wood & Aveluy Wood	4th		The Regt left the front line trenches being relieved by the 1st Wiltshire Regt. and marched to the southern side of AVELUY WOOD where they bivouacked.	
	5th 6th		The Regiment remained in bivouac at Aveluy Wood.	
	7th		At 2pm the regiment marched to ALBERT and remained there for 6 hours and then marched to USNA REDOUBT there being a reserve line of trenches.	
	8th 9th		The Battalion remained at USNA REDOUBT.	
	10th		A & B Companies proceeded to the front line trenches. The Commanding Officer accompanied these two Coys.	
	11th		C & D Coys remained at USNA REDOUBT. A & B in the front line.	

8353 Wt. W2544/1454 700,000 5/15 D. D. & L. A.D.S.S./Forms/C. 2118.

Instructions regarding War Diaries and Intelligence Summaries are contained in F. S. Regs., Part II. and the Staff Manual respectively. Title pages will be prepared in manuscript.

INTELLIGENCE SUMMARY.

(*Erase heading not required.*)

Place	Date	Hour	Summary of Events and Information	Remarks and references to Appendices
	12th		C & D Coys marched at 6pm and joined A & B Coys in the front line taken German trenches.	
OVILLERS.	13th		The Battn was ordered to attack & take two lines of trenches on the southern side of OVILLERS. A & B Coys on the right and C & D on the left. All companies gained their objectives with little resistance. Unfortunately during this operation Capt Carroll A Coy was killed & Lt Rhodes wounded. he eventually died from his wounds.	
	14th		The attack on Ovillers was continued. The trench occupied by C & D Coys was retaken and a block established under Lt Stewart at the Northern end. This trench was then consolidated and held. In the mean time we had pushed forward and taken and held the church and the trench North of it.	
	15th		The XI Cheshire Regt relieved us in the captured trenches. A & B Companies were held in readiness to advance and occupy the trench held by the 2nd S Lancs Regt if they advanced.	

Instructions regarding War Diaries and Intelligence Summaries are contained in F. S. Regs., Part II. and the Staff Manual respectively. Title pages will be prepared in manuscript.

INTELLIGENCE SUMMARY.

(*Erase heading not required.*)

Place	Date	Hour	Summary of Events and Information	Remarks and references to Appendices
Ovillers	16th & 17th		The Battalion rested in the German front line trench which was at this time our support trench to Ovillers. During the night the Battn left the trenches and marched to SENLIS and bivouacked arriving there about 5 am.	
SENLIS	18th		The Regt remained halted till 5 pm when we marched to HEDAUVILLE and bivouacked there for the night	
AMPLIER	19th		Left Hedauville and marched to AMPLIER, billeted in huts.	
"	20		The Brigade was inspected by the Divisional General during the afternoon	
"	21		Baths were allotted to the Battn. Company parades.	
AMPLIER & VAUCHELLES	22		The Battn moved to VAUCHELLES at 10am and were accommodated in huts	
VAUCHELLES & ACHEUX	23rd		Church parade in morning. The Regt moved to ACHEUX at 1pm.	

2353 Wt. W2544/1454 700,000 5/15 D. D. & L. A.D.S.S./Forms/C. 2118.

Instructions regarding War Diaries and Intelligence Summaries are contained in F. S. Regs., Part II. and the Staff Manual respectively. Title pages will be prepared in manuscript.

or

INTELLIGENCE SUMMARY.

(*Erase heading not required.*)

Place	Date	Hour	Summary of Events and Information	Remarks and references to Appendices
ACHEUX	24th		Regiment remained in billets in ACHEUX H	
"	25th		The Regiment moved from ACHEUX to Mailly Wood H	
MAILEY WOOD	26		The regiment remained in Mailly Wood. Draft of 1 Cpl & 97 men arrived H	
	27			
	28		59 men " H	
	29		1 Cpl & 82 men " H	
	30th		The Battalion moved to the front line trenches opposite BEAUMONT HAMEL. Draft of 31 men arrived H	
	31st		Front line trenches. 1 Cpl & 37 men arrived H	

P Strachan Maj
for Lieut-Col
Comdg 8th Border Regt.

2353 Wt. W2544/1454 700,000 5/15 D. D. & L. A.D.S.S./Forms/C. 2118.

A.J. 1S

Hqrs 75th Inf. Bde.

Reference your B.M.O.675 dated 3rd inst.

Right Company during the advance across the open suffered heavy losses from M. Gun Fire.

One of these guns causing the damage was captured by this Coy and put out of action and the detachment of 6 killed. 2 other guns were suspected to be firing from near the Salient in R.31.A.4.2. Touch was lost with the XI Cheshires in the advance. Bombers worked up about 25 yds to the right and a Lewis gun was got into position to cover our right flank. efforts being made to make a temporary block

2

The enemy attacked this post very strongly by Bombing covered by Rifle Fire which enfiladed the enemy front line trench. This caused the ~~enemy~~ right Coy to give way, although bombs were pushed forward as fast as possible they were unable to stop this attack. The Lewis Gun detachment all being killed or wounded. This and a heavy artillery bombardment of the enemy front line and "No Man's Land" were the main cause of having to retire.

Left Coy got over without much difficulty but began to suffer losses from Machine Gun fire from the left. Two dugouts known to be full of Germans were well bombed

3

This Company was getting on very well with the aid of reinforcements but suddenly found that the right flank had given and had to conform. They had already commenced to bomb up the enemies C. Ts and also established a block as they were not in touch with the left Battalion.

This Coy with its reinforcements suffered considerable loss when returning from Machine Gun & Shell fire. Considerable numbers of Casualties were caused in our line while Coys were being reorganised to send back to support line.

There was very little protection from shell fire in our own trenches, as they have been very much damaged by shell fire.

At 3"/4th whilst the stretcher bearers were bringing in the wounded from "No Mans Land" the enemy started throwing Bombs from his front line and opened a heavy Artillery Barrage on all our trenches. It appeared as if he had expected another attack.

This caused a considerable amount of damage. All trenches have been very badly damaged and require a large party for clearing & repairing

C. E. Bond Lt Col
Comdg 8th Border Rgt.

4/7/16

XXV

8 Bardus

Vol 6

6.N.
[illegible]

75th Brigade.

25th Division.

1/8th BATTALION

THE BORDER REGIMENT

AUGUST 1 9 1 6

Instructions regarding War Diaries and Intelligence Summaries are contained in F. S. Regs., Part II. and the Staff Manual respectively. Title pages will be prepared in manuscript.

WAR DIARY
or
INTELLIGENCE SUMMARY.
(*Erase heading not required.*)

Army Form C. 2118.

8TH (SERVICE) BATTALION THE BORDER REGIMENT,

VOL 11

Place	Date 1916 August	Hour	Summary of Events and Information	Remarks and references to Appendices
Front line Trench opposite Beaumont Hamel	1st		The Battalion was employed in constructing new line of trench and improving & repairing existing trenches [initials]	
	2nd 3rd 4th 5th		The Regiment held front line and continued its work on the new trench in North Street & Hunters Trench. The enemy was active with [illegible] & rifle grenades. Total casualties 1 killed and 9 wounded. [initials]	
Bde Reserve	6th		The Battn moved into Brigade Reserve in Trenches 86 and 88. The same working parties were detailed as when in the front line [initials]	
	7th 8 9		Headquarters moved to AUCHONVILLERS. C & D Companies were billeted in the village. A & B Companies remained in 88 and 86 Trench [initials]	10-N [illegible]

#353 Wt. W2544/1454 700,000 5/15 D. D. & L. A.D.S.S./Forms/C. 2118.

Instructions regarding War Diaries and Intelligence Summaries are contained in F. S. Regs., Part II. and the Staff Manual respectively. Title pages will be prepared in manuscript.

WAR DIARY
or
INTELLIGENCE SUMMARY.
(Erase heading not required.)

8TH (SERVICE) BATTALION, THE BORDER REGIMENT.

Army Form C. 2118.

Place	Date	Hour	Summary of Events and Information	Remarks and references to Appendices
AUCHONVILLERS to WARNIMONT WOOD	9th		The Battalion moved into huts at WARNIMONT WOOD being relieved by the Scots Guards & Irish Guards.	
	10th		The Battalion remained in WARNIMONT WOOD.	
	11, 12, 13, 14		The Battalion remained in huts in WARNIMONT WOOD and carried out field training under Company and Battalion arrangements. 2 Officers and 100 men were away on fatigue at COZINCOURT.	
WARNIMONT WOOD & RAINCHEVAL	15		The Battalion moved to RAINCHEVAL during the morning and arrived at their billets about 12.45 pm. The Regt was billeted in the village.	
	16th		Battalion training during morning & afternoon.	
	17th		The Battalion moved to FORCEVILLE	

#353 Wt. W2544/1454 700,000 5/15 D. D. & L. A.D.S.S./Forms/C. 2118.

Army Form C. 2118

Instructions regarding War Diaries and Intelligence Summaries are contained in F. S. Regs., Part II. and the Staff Manual respectively. Title Pages will be prepared in manuscript.

WAR DIARY
or
INTELLIGENCE SUMMARY
(Erase heading not required.)

Place	Date	Hour	Summary of Events and Information	Remarks and references to Appendices
	Aug			
FORCEVILLE	18th		The Battalion left FORCEVILLE at 1pm for AVELUY WOOD. A fatigue party of 300 men & 5 officers were detailed to work on trenches in front line in left sector.	
	19th 20th 21st		The Battalion remained at AVELUY WOOD. Working parties of 400 men were engaged each night from 8.30 pm to 2 am on constructing the 1st parallel in front of the 1st line trench in left sector. Total casualties 1 man of C Coy killed & 4 men wounded.	
	22nd		The Battalion left for HEDAUVILLE. C & D Companies were billeted in the village, A & B Coys in huts in the Chateau grounds.	
	23rd		Company training carried out by the Battalion.	
	24th		Company training carried out by the Battalion.	
	25th		The Battalion left Hedauville at 10pm. B & D Companies with Head Quarters proceeded to the BLUFF via BLACK HORSE BRIDGE. A & C Companies bivouacked the night in AVELUY WOOD.	

1875 Wt. W593/826 1,000,000 4/15 J.B.C. & A. A.D.S.S./Forms/C. 2118.

WAR DIARY
or
INTELLIGENCE SUMMARY
(Erase heading not required.)

Army Form C. 2118

8th (Service) Battalion THE BORDER REGIMENT,

Instructions regarding War Diaries and Intelligence Summaries are contained in F. S. Regs., Part II. and the Staff Manual respectively. Title Pages will be prepared in manuscript.

Place	Date	Hour	Summary of Events and Information	Remarks and references to Appendices
TRENCHES	26th		A & C companies moved at 1.15 pm to QUARRY POST and were joined by B & D companies. The whole battalion then relieved the 1st Battn Wiltshire Regt in the front line trenches. B Coy took over Wiedenberg [?] Trench C & D Coys in support and A Coy in reserve.	
	27th		The front line was heavily shelled throughout the day also the support companies. Many casualties.	
	28th		2nd Lt Hall killed and again many casualties. B Coy relieved by D Coy.	
	29th 30th		The dispositions of Companies the same. The whole line was heavily shelled day & night. Lt Renton [?] was killed & 2nd Lt Key [?] was wounded. Many casualties.	
	31st		A Coy relieved D company in the front line.	

2/9/16

[illegible signature] Major for Lt Col
Comdg. 8th Border Regiment

1875 Wt. W593/826 1,000,000 4/15 J.B.C. & A. A.D.S.S./Forms/C. 2118.

75th. INFANTRY BDE.

25th. DIVISION

8th. B O R D E R   R E G T.

S E P T E M B E R   1 9 1 6.

Army Form C. 2118

Instructions regarding War Diaries and Intelligence Summaries are contained in F. S. Regs., Part II. and the Staff Manual respectively. Title Pages will be prepared in manuscript.

WAR DIARY
or
INTELLIGENCE SUMMARY
(Erase heading not required.)

8/BORDER RGT. Vol 12
SEPT 1916

Place	Date	Hour	Summary of Events and Information	Remarks and references to Appendices
TRENCHES – BOUZINCOURT	Sept. 1st		At 2 am. the Battalion was relieved by the 2nd Cheshire Regt. The relief was not completed till 8 am. The Regiment went into billets at BOUZINCOURT. Inspected by the G.O.C. at 6 pm. At 8.30 pm the officers & N.C.O.s witnessed a practice attack by the 1st Wiltshire Regt.	
	2nd		The Battalion left BOUZINCOURT at 2.45 pm & went into front line trench (HINDENBURG TRENCH) relieving 8th S. Lancs Regt.	
	3rd 4th 5th 6th		In front line trenches at LEIPZIG SALIENT. The Battn was engaged in holding these trenches and improving & repairing them. Fewer casualties than when they were held before.	
	7th		The Battn was relieved during the morning by the West Riding Regt and marched to BOUZINCOURT where they were billeted for the night.	

1875 Wt. W593/826 1,000,000 4/15 J.B.C. & A. A.D.S.S./Forms/C. 2118.

11. N.

Instructions regarding War Diaries and Intelligence Summaries are contained in F. S. Regs., Part II. and the Staff Manual respectively. Title Pages will be prepared in manuscript.

WAR DIARY
or
INTELLIGENCE SUMMARY
(Erase heading not required.)

Army Form C. 2118

Place	Date	Hour	Summary of Events and Information	Remarks and references to Appendices
BOUZINCOURT	8th		The Battalion marched to LILLEVILLERS to billets.	
LILLEVILLERS	9th		The Regt remained at LILLEVILLERS. 5 officers proceeded to AMIENS for the day.	
AMPLIER	10th		Marched to AMPLIER and billeted in huts.	
	11th		Marched to VACQUERIE	
DOMLEGER	12th		The Battalion proceeded to DOMLEGER.	
"	13th		The day was given up to cleaning equipment etc and refitting.	
"	14		Squad drill, company training, Bayonet fighting and physical drill. 6 hours per day.	
	15			
	16			
"	17th		Church parade at 10 am. Three officers attended for demonstration	
"	18th		Indoor work, lectures etc. Five officers attended for demonstration	

1875 Wt. W593/826 1,000,000 4/15 J.B.C. & A. A.D.S.S./Forms/C. 2118.

Army Form C. 2118

WAR DIARY
or
INTELLIGENCE SUMMARY
(Erase heading not required.)

Instructions regarding War Diaries and Intelligence Summaries are contained in F. S. Regs., Part II. and the Staff Manual respectively. Title Pages will be prepared in manuscript.

Place	Date	Hour	Summary of Events and Information	Remarks and references to Appendices
Domleger	19.		Company training one Company on the range.	
	20.		— do — one Company on the range.	
	21.		— do — Lectures on Gas, one Company on range.	
	22.		— do — Lectures on Bayonet Fighting & Discipline.	
	23.		— do — in morning Football Competition 2nd South Lancs Borders winning by 3 goals to 1. Orders to move 6.	
	24		Church Parade. Preparations for move.	
	25		Moved to Amplier starting at 7 a.m. Halted for one hour & ½ at midday. Total Distance 16½ miles. Very few men fell out.	
Amplier	26		Marched to Lealvillers. Good few men fell out owing to heat.	
Lealvillers	27		2 Coys A&B. were practised in Intrenching digging by R.E. Other Coys practised Bayonet fighting. Lectures were given to Coys by Coy Commanders. NCOs under RSM in afternoon.	

1875 Wt. W593/826 1,000,000 4/15 J.B.C. & A. A.D.S.S./Forms/C. 2118.

Instructions regarding War Diaries and Intelligence Summaries are contained in F. S. Regs., Part II. and the Staff Manual respectively. Title Pages will be prepared in manuscript.

Army Form C. 2118

WAR DIARY
or
INTELLIGENCE SUMMARY
(Erase heading not required.)

Place	Date	Hour	Summary of Events and Information	Remarks and references to Appendices
Lealvillers	28		2 Coys were practised in intensive digging (C & D) Lecture by Lt.Col. E. H. Birch G.S.O. 1 Division on Lessons learnt on operations since July 1st. All Coy Officers C.O. Adjt B.O. & M.G.O attended [initials]	
"	29		Moved to Bivouacs in field just N.E of BOUZINCOURT no men fell out on march. [initials]	
"	30		Moved to Dugouts in Ovillers [initials]	
~~[illegible]~~ ~~Ovillers~~	~~[illegible]~~		~~Bombardment in Ovillers at 3.15 heavy bombardment by our guns opened. Informed that Canadians were attacking.~~ [initials]	

C. E. Bond Lt. Col.
Comdg 8th Border Regt

75th Inf. Bde.

25th Division

8th Battn.

BORDER REGIMENT,

O C T O B E R, 1 9 1 6.

Instructions regarding War Diaries and Intelligence Summaries are contained in F. S. Regs., Part II. and the Staff Manual respectively. Title Pages will be prepared in manuscript.

WAR DIARY
or
INTELLIGENCE SUMMARY
(Erase heading not required.)

8th Border Regt.

Army Form C. 2118

Vol 13

Place	Date	Hour	Summary of Events and Information	Remarks and references to Appendices
Ovillers Trenches	Oct 1		In Dugouts in old German Front line and North side of Road. Working parties supplied for carrying rations & stores up to Mouquet Farm	
	2		— do —	
	3		— do —	
	4		— do — Lt Parkinson hit in leg.	
	5		— do — Ordered to relieve Canadians on right of Pozieres. In relief 2 Lieut Turner was wounded.	
Trenches	6		Trenches were shelled intermittently shelled throughout the day. CSM of D Coy killed. 2 Lt Lewis wounded & 2 Lt. Wilson. Relieved by the 9th L.N.L. 76th Brigade & Proceeded to ~~Crucifix~~ Crucifix Corner.	
Crucifix Corner	7		Men cleaning up after Trenches.	12-N. 9 sheets

1875 Wt. W593/826 1,000,000 4/15 J.B.C. & A. A.D.S.S./Forms/C. 2118.

Army Form C. 2118

Instructions regarding War Diaries and Intelligence Summaries are contained in F. S. Regs., Part II. and the Staff Manual respectively. Title Pages will be prepared in manuscript.

WAR DIARY
or
INTELLIGENCE SUMMARY
(Erase heading not required.)

Place	Date	Hour	Summary of Events and Information	Remarks and references to Appendices
[illegible] Corner	8.		Companies under Coy arrangement. Bayonet Fighting Bomb throwing &c. H	
	9		— do — H	
	10		— do — N. C. Os proceeded in afternoon to look at ground over which an attack was to be practised on next day.	
	11		Attack Practiced 1st by Coy & then by Battalion Major Strahan in Command. H	
	12th		Company & Battalion training H	
	13th		Battalion training. H	

W. W3092/P6 1,000,000 4/15 J.B.C. & A. A.D.S.S./Forms/C. 2118.

Instructions regarding War Diaries and Intelligence Summaries are contained in F. S. Regs., Part II. and the Staff Manual respectively. Title Pages will be prepared in manuscript.

WAR DIARY
or
INTELLIGENCE SUMMARY
(Erase heading not required.)

Army Form C. 2118

Place	Date	Hour	Summary of Events and Information	Remarks and references to Appendices
Courcelette Corner	14th		The O.C. and Coy officers inspected the line of trenches to be taken up by the Battn.	
Stuff Redoubt	15th		The Battn relieved the 1st Wilts Regt in the front line. We were the left Battn in the Division, the 39th being on our left, the 2nd S Lancs Regt on our right. During the evening the headquarters were heavily bombarded.	
	16th		The Battn moved to the right, taking the line occupied by the 2nd S. Lancs Regt. HQ moved to Quarry Pit.	
	17th 18th		Battn engaged in repairing & strengthening their line.	
	19th		The contemplated attack on Regina Trench postponed 48 hours on account of rain. Lt Parmenter wounded.	
	20th		Repairing of trenches after the rain continued.	

1875 Wt. W593/826 1,000,000 4/15 J.B.C. & A. A.D.S.S./Forms/C. 2118.

Instructions regarding War Diaries and Intelligence Summaries are contained in F. S. Regs., Part II. and the Staff Manual respectively. Title Pages will be prepared in manuscript.

WAR DIARY
or
INTELLIGENCE SUMMARY
(Erase heading not required.)

Army Form C. 2118

Place	Date	Hour	Summary of Events and Information	Remarks and references to Appendices
Stuff Redoubt	21st		Attack on REGINA TRENCH by the Battn and 1 Coy of 11th Cheshire Regt. The Battn and 1 Coy XI Cheshires took over the line in Hessian trench at 6am the relief being completed by 8am. Borders on right & Cheshires on left of line. The objective in Regina Trench assigned to the Battn was roughly 350 yards the 13th Cheshires 74th Bde being on our right & responsible for the [illegible] [illegible] the 8th S Lancs were on our left. The attack was advanced in four waves, Borders being in ½ Coy columns Along [?] XIth Cheshires in columns of platoons 30 paces distance. Our artillery barrage opened at 12.6 pm which was the signal to get out of the trench: the waves were not very good but there was no confusion, direction was well kept by the Borders, this was caused by the communication trench on the right running obliquely across our front, a change of direction had also to be made. The whole advanced too quickly, sufficient attention was not paid to the barrage orders, officers were few, but watches could not have been properly used.	

1875 Wt. W593/826 1,000,000 4/15 J.B.C. & A. A.D.S.S./Forms/C. 2118.

Instructions regarding War Diaries and Intelligence Summaries are contained in F. S. Regs., Part II. and the Staff Manual respectively. Title Pages will be prepared in manuscript.

WAR DIARY
or
INTELLIGENCE SUMMARY
(Erase heading not required.)

Army Form C. 2118

Place	Date	Hour	Summary of Events and Information	Remarks and references to Appendices
Stuff Redoubt	21st (cont)		The ground was not cut up by shell holes as much as was expected and was easy to advance over, the leading wave reached the objective before the barrage lifted and suffered some casualties in consequence, the wire was well cut and presented no obstacle. The barrage was excellent, a few shells were short, but I think this must be expected. The attack was sudden and swift, had there been a slight check to allow the barrage to lift the Battn would have got over almost without a casualty. When the trench was reached on the left, the men got in so easily that they did not realize they had gained their objective, a gap was also left on the right owing to opposition from a Large dugout on the right where a machine gun fired a few rounds. Some dugouts & emplacements showed up very plainly on the left of STUMP ROAD and Germans were seen coming out of them within a minute of reaching REGINA TRENCH some officer & about 80 men of whom 40 were Bombers left the trench and made	

1875 Wt. W593/826 1,000,000 4/15 J.B.C. & A. A.D.S.S./Forms/C. 2118.

Instructions regarding War Diaries and Intelligence Summaries are contained in F. S. Regs., Part II. and the Staff Manual respectively. Title Pages will be prepared in manuscript.

WAR DIARY
or
INTELLIGENCE SUMMARY
(Erase heading not required.)

Army Form C. 2118

Place	Date	Hour	Summary of Events and Information	Remarks and references to Appendices
Stuff Redoubt	21st		straight across for them. Amongst these men were about 20 of the 13th Cheshires who had come across our front, some went through the Hun lines & occupied a trench some 600 yds in front of the line, they were withdrawn after dark. Capt Stewart realized what was happening and stopped a good many from going forward and got them to work at once in the trench. He found he was in touch with the 8th S. Lancs on the left but the right was held up. He ordered a block to be made till he could collect some more men as the line was thin & sent back a written report of the situation which was most useful as it arrived soon after a report came from Lt Aitken(?) as to the situation on the right. He said the trench had not been cleared but was full of Borders & Cheshires; this turned out to be the bombers originally told off to clear the right & two details of Lewis guns & about 30 men of the Cheshire Regt who were unable to get on. Lt Birnie(?) was then sent up with the last remaining squad of Batt Bombers at Batt HQ to try and get touch with Capt Stewart by bombing up the CT. On arriving at the dug out he found that the one just beyond the block was ablaze and he could not get on that way but under cover of the smoke caused by it he managed to get his squad & 10 others from the CT over mass of men to th	

1875 Wt. W593/826 1,000,000 4/15 J.B.C. & A. A.D.S.S./Forms/C. 2118.

Army Form C. 2118

WAR DIARY
or
INTELLIGENCE SUMMARY
(Erase heading not required.)

Instructions regarding War Diaries and Intelligence Summaries are contained in F. S. Regs., Part II. and the Staff Manual respectively. Title Pages will be prepared in manuscript.

Place	Date	Hour	Summary of Events and Information	Remarks and references to Appendices
Stuff Redoubt	21st		to Regina Trench to where Capt Stewart was, only one man being hit on the way. He got to work at once in a very gallant manner himself getting on to the parapet and sniping while his men worked up the trench, he accounted for at least 8 Germans killed, and within 20 minutes the remainder about 60 surrendered, the trench was cleared and touch gained with the 13th Cheshires. Consolidation proceeded without opposition and several patrols were captured during the night. 3 machine guns were captured, 1 by the Borders 1 by XIth Cheshires & 1 by the 8 Lancs, 251 Germans were captured and 50 killed were counted. The Coy of the XIth Cheshire Regt & the officers attached from that Battn rendered very useful assistance. Also the platoon of carriers who did excellent work carrying bombs and ammunition.	
			A Coy of the XIth Cheshires was ordered to reinforce the front line, their place in Hessian Trench being taken by 1 Coy Xth Cheshires.	
			FIELD TRENCH was dug during the night by the R.Es also the CT on the right was improved and made passable throughout [illegible]	

Instructions regarding War Diaries and Intelligence Summaries are contained in F. S. Regs., Part II. and the Staff Manual respectively. Title Pages will be prepared in manuscript.

WAR DIARY
or
INTELLIGENCE SUMMARY
(Erase heading not required.)

Army Form C. 2118

Place	Date	Hour	Summary of Events and Information	Remarks and references to Appendices
Stuff Redoubt	21st		This trench was heavily shelled very soon after the attack commenced, this was kept up intermittently for 24 hours until the Batt. was relieved.	
			The front line was thinned out on the morning of the 22nd the Coy of X1th Cheshires being sent back to their HQ, the X1th Cheshires from front line taking their place. The bombers of the X1th Cheshires were kept in reserve and were not required. Casualties Capt Miller & Capt Watson Thomas (killed) Lt Le May wounded. 18 other ranks killed 111 wounded 30 missing.	
	22nd		Batt relieved by the 10th Worcesters & marched to camp between Albert & Bouzincourt	
	23rd		Batt left camp and went to Warloy in motor busses.	
Gezaincourt	24th		Batt left Warloy & marched to Gezaincourt some went by road and some in busses	
"	25th		The Corps Commander inspected the Brigade. The Borders & 2nd Lancs paraded at 2 pm in the Chateau grounds.	

1875 Wt. W593/826 1,000,000 4/15 J.B.C. & A. A.D.S.S./Forms/C. 2118.

Army Form C. 2118

WAR DIARY
or
INTELLIGENCE SUMMARY
(Erase heading not required.)

Instructions regarding War Diaries and Intelligence Summaries are contained in F. S. Regs., Part II. and the Staff Manual respectively. Title Pages will be prepared in manuscript.

Place	Date	Hour	Summary of Events and Information	Remarks and references to Appendices
Gezaincourt	27th		The Battn was unable to carry out field training on account of the bad weather. Sir Douglas Haig inspected the Battn in billets during the afternoon.	
"	28th		Training was carried on under Company arrangements.	
"	29th		Church parade at 9.30. At 7 pm the Battn left Gezaincourt for Doullens to entrain for Bailleul. Train left at 10.50 pm.	
Meteren	30th		The Battn arrived by train at Bailleul at 5 am, and detrained and marched to Meteren.	
	31st		Company training carried out. O.C. Battn [illegible] proceeded to Romarin to inspect part of new line being taken over by the Brigade.	

J. Strahan Major

1875 Wt. W593/826 1,000,000 4/15 J.B.C. & A. A.D.S.S./Forms/C. 2118.

75th Inf. Bde.

25th Division

8th Battn.

BORDER REGIMENT,

N O V E M B E R, 1 9 1 6.

Instructions regarding War Diaries and Intelligence Summaries are contained in F. S. Regs., Part II. and the Staff Manual respectively. Title Pages will be prepared in manuscript.

WAR DIARY
or
INTELLIGENCE SUMMARY
(Erase heading not required.)

Army Form C. 2118

8 Border Regt

Vol ~~8~~ 14

Place	Date	Hour	Summary of Events and Information	Remarks and references to Appendices
Pont de Nieppe	Nov 1st		The Regiment moved to Pont de Nieppe. B and A Companies billeted at the Divisional Baths and C & D Coys in Nieppe.	
	2nd		Moved at midday to huts in Romarin.	
Romarin	3rd		Company training. Draft of 42 men arrived & two officers.	
	4th			
	5th		Church parade in morning.	
	6th		Company training. Draft of 22 men arrived. 1 officer.	
	7th			
Trenches	8th		The Battalion relieved [illegible] Cheshires in front line trenches. The 12th R. Irish Rifles on our left and the 8th South Lancs on our right. Our line extending from the R. Douve to Seaforth Farm. HQ of Battn at Red Lodge. D Coy in front line. C " Subsidiary line. A " Support & Bn Reserve.	13. N. 57 sheets

1875 Wt. W593/826 1,000,000 4/15 J.B.C. & A. A.D.S.S./Forms/C. 2118.

Instructions regarding War Diaries and Intelligence Summaries are contained in F. S. Regs., Part II. and the Staff Manual respectively. Title Pages will be prepared in manuscript.

WAR DIARY
or
INTELLIGENCE SUMMARY
(Erase heading not required.)

Army Form C. 2118

Place	Date	Hour	Summary of Events and Information	Remarks and references to Appendices
Trenches	9th		Quiet day. Coys engaged in repairing & improving trenches. Patrols had nothing special to report.	
	10th		The Subsidiary line had a few hostile shells. The usual work was carried on. 20 men from the X. Cheshire Regt were sent to help to repair front line.	
	11th		D Coy in front line was relieved by B Coy. The remaining two Coys were not moved.	
	12th		Quiet day. The front line received about 6 shells (small) on the front line. Fatigue parties carried up material during the night.	
	13th		The enemy again shelled front line also the Subsidiary line. Repair work was carried on without trouble & the usual fatigue parties carried up material.	
	14th		The Battalion was relieved in the front line trenches by the XI Cheshires	

1875 Wt. W593/826 1,000,000 4/15 J.B.C. & A. A.D.S.S./Forms/C. 2118.

Instructions regarding War Diaries and Intelligence Summaries are contained in F. S. Regs., Part II. and the Staff Manual respectively. Title Pages will be prepared in manuscript.

WAR DIARY
or
INTELLIGENCE SUMMARY
(Erase heading not required.)

Army Form C. 2118

Place	Date	Hour	Summary of Events and Information	Remarks and references to Appendices
Trenches	15th		The new draft of 125 men were drilled and instructed during the morning. Fort Marshall & Brenda were taken over and repairs started. Each fort held of 1 NCO and 7 men.	
	16		All available men were practised in the use of the new box gas respirators. 30 men in the morning & 31 in the afternoon were sent up to front line as working parties & 30 men as carrying party and 20 as working party at night in fr trench.	
	17th		The Battalion furnished the same parties as on the 16th also 21 men to work on Forts Marshall & Brenda.	
	18		Same as 17th	
	19			
	20th		The Battalion relieved the 1st Cheshires in the trenches. A Coy front line. B " Subsidiary line	

Instructions regarding War Diaries and Intelligence Summaries are contained in F. S. Regs., Part II. and the Staff Manual respectively. Title Pages will be prepared in manuscript.

WAR DIARY
or
INTELLIGENCE SUMMARY
(Erase heading not required.)

Army Form C. 2118

Place	Date	Hour	Summary of Events and Information	Remarks and references to Appendices
Trenches	20th		C Coy in support D Coy in Subsidiary & Locality 3.	
"	21st 22nd		Nothing of importance to relate. The usual working parties carried out repairs in the front line & C.T.	
"	23rd		B & C Coy relieved A Coy in the front line. About 12 shells were fired into the front line area by the Germans, no damage	
	24 25		Repairs were carried out in front line & subsidiary line	
	26th		The Battn was relieved by the XI Cheshires. Forts Marshall and Brandon occupied by detachments from A Coy.	
Red Lodge	27th 28th		The Battn was exercised under Coy arrangements in drill, bayonet fighting, Physical Exercises. 200 men each day were sent up to the firing line to help the XIth Cheshires repair parapets.	

1875 Wt. W593/826 1,000,000 4/15 J.B.C. & A. A.D.S.S./Forms/C. 2118.

Instructions regarding War Diaries and Intelligence Summaries are contained in F. S. Regs., Part II. and the Staff Manual respectively. Title Pages will be prepared in manuscript.

WAR DIARY
or
INTELLIGENCE SUMMARY

(Erase heading not required.)

Army Form C. 2118

Place	Date	Hour	Summary of Events and Information	Remarks and references to Appendices
Red Lodge	29th		The two detachments in Forts Brandon and Marshall were relieved by two more detachments of A Coy. The usual fatigue parties were furnished.	
	30th		The usual working parties were furnished to assist in repairing the front line trench. The remainder of the Batt. was exercised in drill bayonet fighting & physical exercises.	

C. E. Bond Lt Col.

1875 Wt. W593/826 1,000,000 4/15 J.B.C. & A. A.D.S.S./Forms/C. 2118.

75th Inf. Bde.

25th Division

8th Battn.

BORDER REGIMENT,

D E C E M B E R, 1 9 1 6.

Instructions regarding War Diaries and Intelligence Summaries are contained in F. S. Regs., Part II. and the Staff Manual respectively. Title Pages will be prepared in manuscript.

WAR DIARY
or
INTELLIGENCE SUMMARY
(Erase heading not required.)

Army Form C. 2118

8 Border Regt

Vol 15

Place	Date Dec	Hour	Summary of Events and Information	Remarks and references to Appendices
Red Lodge	1st		The Battn still holding front line trenches. Parties from XI Cheshire Regt sent up during the morning & afternoon to assist in repair of parapets.	
	2nd		The front line occupied by B Coy was shelled during the morning between 11 & 12 no damage or casualties	
	3rd		Quiet day nothing to report.	
	4th		No working parties were supplied by the XI Cheshires. The repairs to the subsidiary line were carried out by A Coy.	
	5th		The Battn was relieved by the 12th South Wales during the morning and afternoon and moved to the subsector in Ploegsteert Wood. Battn HQ were situated at Custom farm. A Coy at Tongue Rouge B & C Coy at Ploegsteert Hall and D Coy in [illegible] line	
	6th		The day was given up to cleaning of Equipment etc and baths	
	7th		Training was carried out under Company arrangements	
	8th		D Coy in the front line was relieved by C Coy.	

14.N. 6 sheets

1875 Wt. W593/826 1,000,000 4/15 J.B.C. & A. A.D.S.S./Forms/C. 2118.

Instructions regarding War Diaries and Intelligence Summaries are contained in F. S. Regs., Part II. and the Staff Manual respectively. Title Pages will be prepared in manuscript.

WAR DIARY
or
INTELLIGENCE SUMMARY
(Erase heading not required.)

Army Form C. 2118

Place	Date	Hour	Summary of Events and Information	Remarks and references to Appendices
	Dec			
Ploegsteert	9th		Training was continued under Company arrangement.	
	10th		The Battn relieved XI Cheshire Regt in front line trenches. C Coy on the left B Coy in the centre and A on the right. D Coy in support line. The XIII Cheshire on our left and 8th S Lancs Regt on our right.	
	11th		Work was carried out in repairing parapets and improving trenches.	
	12th		Quiet day nothing to report.	
	13th		B Coy was relieved by C Coy in the centre of the line.	
	14th		The Brigadier inspected the line during the morning.	
	15th		Quiet day nothing to report.	
	16th		Battn relieved by XI Cheshire Regt. The regt went into huts at ROMARIN on being relieved.	
	17th		Battn cleaning equipment & clothing.	

1875 Wt. W593/826 1,000,000 4/15 J.B.C. & A. A.D.S.S./Forms/C. 2118.

Instructions regarding War Diaries and Intelligence Summaries are contained in F. S. Regs., Part II. and the Staff Manual respectively. Title Pages will be prepared in manuscript.

WAR DIARY
or
INTELLIGENCE SUMMARY
(Erase heading not required.)

Army Form C. 2118

Place	Date	Hour	Summary of Events and Information	Remarks and references to Appendices
Romarin	18th		The Battn was exercised in Company training, Physical exercises and bayonet fighting.	
	19th		One company (A) proceeded to Meteren to undergo instruction in wiring. The remaining 3 companies practised wiring at Romarin.	
	20th		The regiment was inspected by Genl Sir Douglas Haig during the morning.	
	21st		The Battalion had a route march under company arrangement distance 7½ miles.	
	22nd		The Battalion relieved 1st Cheshire Regt during the morning in the front line trenches. The 1st Cheshires on our left and 8th South Lancs on our right. C Coy on left of line D in centre and A on the right B Coy being in support. During the afternoon A Coy was shelled by the enemy, considerable damage being done.	

1875 Wt. W593/826 1,000,000 4/15 J.B.C. & A. A.D.S.S./Forms/C. 2118.

Instructions regarding War Diaries and Intelligence Summaries are contained in F. S. Regs., Part II. and the Staff Manual respectively. Title Pages will be prepared in manuscript.

WAR DIARY
or
INTELLIGENCE SUMMARY
(Erase heading not required.)

Army Form C. 2118

Place	Date	Hour	Summary of Events and Information	Remarks and references to Appendices
Trenches	23rd		A Coy was again subjected to considerable shell fire, also heavy trench mortar and aerial torpedoes, 1 man was killed and one wounded. A great deal of damage was inflicted on our parapet.	
"	24th		A quiet day with the exception of intermittent shelling on our right Coy. A Coy was temporarily relieved by C Coy.	
	25th		A Coy again took its place on the right of the line. A successful raid was carried out by the XI Cheshires Regt on the German line opposite the front held by A Coy. The artillery barrage opened at 8.20 and almost immediately the party of the XI Cheshires entered the German trenches. They came back with only the loss of 1 man killed. They killed a considerable number of the enemy & brought back one prisoner. Our casualties were 8 men wounded 5 seriously.	
	26th		The companies were engaged in repairing the parapets damaged.	

1875 Wt. W593/826 1,000,000 4/15 J.B.C. & A. A.D.S.S./Forms/C. 2118.

Army Form C. 2118

Instructions regarding War Diaries and Intelligence Summaries are contained in F. S. Regs., Part II. and the Staff Manual respectively. Title Pages will be prepared in manuscript.

WAR DIARY
or
INTELLIGENCE SUMMARY
(Erase heading not required.)

Place	Date	Hour	Summary of Events and Information	Remarks and references to Appendices
	Dec			
Trenches	26th		of the German artillery fire. We had one man badly wounded. [initials]	
	27th		A quiet day. Very little shelling from either side. Our casualties was one man seriously wounded. (since died). [initials]	
	28th		The Battalion was relieved in the front line by the xi Cheshire Regt. A Coy at Touquet Berthe. B Coy in front line. C & D at Ploegsteert Hill [initials]	
	29th		The new draft of 270 men were inspected during the morning. The remainder of the Battn engaged in cleaning up. [initials]	
	30th		Detachment of new draft paraded during the morning for drill & exercises. Working parties furnished by the remaining companies. The Battn was practised in a "night alarm" [initials]	
	31st		Church parade in the morning. B Coy relieved by D Coy in the front line. [initials]	

P. Strahan Maj
Cmdg 8th Batt Border Regt

1875 Wt. W593/826 1,000,000 4/15 J.B.C. & A. A.D.S.S./Forms/C. 2118.

MOVE ORDERS. SECRET.

1. The Battalion will be relieved by the 14th. R. I. Rs. tomorrow the 5th. Instant.

2. Four Guides per Company and one from Battalion Headquarters will report to R. S. M. at 11-30 a.m. at Red Lodge.

3. Coys. on relief will vacate their present positions by the ONLY WAY, and will proceed to the new area taking up the following positions there:-

"A" Coy. Touquet Berth.
"B" Coy.) Ploegsteert Hall.
"C" Coy.)
"D" Coy.-Fort Line.

C. Q. M. S.s. will meet their Coys. at Hyde Park Corner and will guide them to their respective positions as shown above.

4. All drums of Lewis Gun Ammunition will be handed over to the relieving Battalion. The Lewis Gun Officer will ascertain from the L. G. O. of the relieving Battalion The exact number of magazines he is to hand over.

5. Transport Officer will arrange to have one Limber for L. G. Magazines, One limber for cooks stores, one G. S. Wagon for blankets, one G. S. Wagon for Officers kits, and mess cart at Headquarters at 2-30 p.m. All Officers kits, mess stores, blankets and Orderly Room boxes to be at Hqrs. Red Lodge by 2-30 p.m. The above will be transported to point where the Strand meets the Ploegsteert-Hyde Park Corner Road, except Headquarters which will be taken on to CRESLOW.

6. Coys. will report relief complete as soon as they arrive in their new quarters by the word "DUD".

7. Battalion Headquarters will move to Creslow as soon as Headquarters of relieving Battalion have taken over. They will march under the R. S. M. who will arrange to reconnoitre the accomodation before hand. The R. S. M. will hand over and obtain receipts for all trench stores under his charge.

8. All Gum-Boots will be sent down to Headquarters and handed over to the pioneer sergeant by 11 a.m. Pioneer Sergt. will then hand these over to the Gum-Boot Store obtaining receipt for the full complement used by the Battalion.

9. Coys when handing over will give as much information about the sector as possible to the Officers of the relieving Unit. All maps, documents, (except Code Books) and trench stores will be handed over and receipts taken-copies of which will be forwarded to Battalion Headquarters by 9 a.m. 6th. inst.

10. If there is no Unit to take over from in the new area an inventory of all ammunition, trench stores, documents etc. will be forwarded to Headquarters by 6 p.m. 6th. inst.

11. ACKNOWLEDGE.

..............................Capt. & Adjut.,

4/12/16. 8th. Border Regiment.

Instructions regarding War Diaries and Intelligence Summaries are contained in F. S. Regs., Part II. and the Staff Manual respectively. Title Pages will be prepared in manuscript.

WAR DIARY or ~~INTELLIGENCE SUMMARY~~

8th Border Regt.

(Erase heading not required.)

Army Form C. 2118

Vol 16

Place	Date Jan	Hour	Summary of Events and Information	Remarks and references to Appendices
Trenches PLOEGSTEERT	1st		Quiet day nothing to report	
NIL	2nd		The Battn left the line and came into billet at NIEPPE for a fortnights training	
	3rd		Cleaning billets, rifles, equipment etc.	
	4th		A Coy was on 30 yds range all day. The remaining Coys underwent instruction in wiring under R.E. Officer.	
	5th		B Coy on the range at ROMARIN. The remainder of the Battn did Bayonet fighting Physical drill etc.	
	6th		The same as the 5th, in addition extended order drill was practised and a lecture given by MO in the evening.	
	7th		Church Parade and Recreation	
	8th		C & D Companies marched to the training ground at BAILLEUL and practised the attack by Companies. Remaining Coys, bayonet fighting	15 N. 5 sheets

1875 Wt. W593/826 1,000,000 4/15 J.B.C. & A. A.D.S.S./Forms/C. 2118.

Instructions regarding War Diaries and Intelligence Summaries are contained in F. S. Regs., Part II. and the Staff Manual respectively. Title Pages will be prepared in manuscript.

WAR DIARY
or
INTELLIGENCE SUMMARY
(Erase heading not required.)

Army Form C. 2118

Place	Date	Hour	Summary of Events and Information	Remarks and references to Appendices
			Physical drill, extended order drill and musketry exercises.	
NIEPPE	9th		C Company on the range at NIEPPE remaining Coys as on the 8th.	
	10th		A & B Companies marched to the training ground at BAILLEUL and practised the attack. [illegible] Companies	
	11th		D Company on the range, remaining Coys. bayonet exercises etc.	
	12th		The Battalion marched to BAILLEUL and practised the attack.	
	13th		The Battalion started to march to the training ground for practice attack in Brigade, but ordered to return on account of bad weather.	
	14th		Church parade & recreation. 8th Borders beat [illegible] in 1st round for cup at football.	
	15th		The Brigade marched to the training ground and practised the attack.	
	16th		The day given up to cleaning billets, equipment etc. Final football played in afternoon 8th Borders beat 8 S Lancs 2 goals to 0.	

1875 Wt. W593/826 1,000,000 4/15 J.B.C. & A. A.D.S.S./Forms/C. 2118.

Instructions regarding War Diaries and Intelligence Summaries are contained in F. S. Regs., Part II. and the Staff Manual respectively. Title Pages will be prepared in manuscript.

WAR DIARY
or
INTELLIGENCE SUMMARY
(Erase heading not required.)

Army Form C. 2118

Place	Date	Hour	Summary of Events and Information	Remarks and references to Appendices
	Jan			
NIEPPE	17th		The Battn was relieved by the 10th Cheshire Regt at NIEPPE and marched to PONT DE NIEPPE and relieved the 1st Wilts Regt	
PONT DE NIEPPE	18th		Five carrying parties numbering 170 men were supplied by the Battn for carrying material to the trenches. H	
	19th 20th 21st		During these days the Battn furnished the same carrying parties as on the 18th. The remainder were exercised in bayonet fighting, physical drill, semaphore training & route marching. H	
	22nd		The Battn was ordered at 6pm to hold itself in readiness to proceed to the trenches as the Germans made a raid on the front held by the 74th Brigade. H	
Trenches	23rd		The Battn relieved the 10th Cheshire Regt in the front line trenches. B Coy on the right, D in the centre & A Coy on the left. C Coy being in support at TANCREZ FARM. [The 8th S Lancs were on our left, and the Australians on our right) the river Lys being the dividing line. H	

1875 Wt. W593/826 1,000,000 4/15 J.B.C. & A. A.D.S.S./Forms/C. 2118.

Instructions regarding War Diaries and Intelligence Summaries are contained in F. S. Regs., Part II. and the Staff Manual respectively. Title Pages will be prepared in manuscript.

WAR DIARY
or
INTELLIGENCE SUMMARY

(Erase heading not required.)

Army Form C. 2118

Place	Date	Hour	Summary of Events and Information	Remarks and references to Appendices
Trenches	Jan 24th		Fairly quiet day. No casualties. Severe frost.	
	26th		Very little work could be carried out on account of the frost. The 3 Companies in the front line were engaged in wiring.	
	26th		About 3 pm the Germans opened heavy artillery fire on TOURET STATION, little damage was done & no casualties.	
	27th		A quiet day, all companies engaged in strengthening their posts. Frost still too severe for other work.	
	28th		The German artillery more active than yesterday, one man wounded by shrapnel bullet. Usual wiring was carried out.	
	29th		The Battn was relieved by the XI Cheshires, and went to LE BIZET and were distributed as follows. 2 Companies in LE BIZET. One company (B) occupied LANCASHIRE SUPPORT FARM, RESERVE FARM and GUNNERS FARM.	968?

1875 Wt. W593/826 1,000,000 4/15 J.B.C. & A. A.D.S.S./Forms/C. 2118.

Instructions regarding War Diaries and Intelligence Summaries are contained in F. S. Regs., Part II. and the Staff Manual respectively. Title Pages will be prepared in manuscript.

WAR DIARY
or
INTELLIGENCE SUMMARY
(Erase heading not required.)

Army Form C. 2118

Place	Date	Hour	Summary of Events and Information	Remarks and references to Appendices
Trenches	29th		One company (C) occupied LYS FARM, STATION REDOUBT, and SEVEN TREES REDOUBT.	
	30th		The Battn engaged in cleaning arms, equipment, & clothing.	
	31st		85 men were employed in carrying materials up to the front line trenches, the remainder practiced bomb throwing, physical exercise & bayonet fighting.	

P Shakar Maj
8th Battn Border Regt

9691
E.B.

1875 Wt. W593/826 1,000,000 4/15 J.B.C. & A. A.D.S.S./Forms/C. 2118.

Instructions regarding War Diaries and Intelligence Summaries are contained in F. S. Regs., Part II. and the Staff Manual respectively. Title Pages will be prepared in manuscript.

WAR DIARY
or
INTELLIGENCE SUMMARY
(Erase heading not required.)

8th Border Regt

Army Form C. 2118

Vol 17

Place	Date Feb	Hour	Summary of Events and Information	Remarks and references to Appendices
LEBIZET & SUPPORT LANE	1st		The Battn furnished the usual carrying parties to the front line. A few shells fell in the village to the South of Battn HQ.	
	2nd		Extra carrying parties were required to carry up material to front line in anticipation of a thaw.	
	3rd			
Trenches	4th		The Battn relieved the 11th Cheshires in the trenches taking over the same portion of the line as in the last tour. A Coy on left, D in centre and C on the right. B in support at Tancrez Farm.	
	5th		Quiet day nothing to report.	
	6th		The Companies were engaged in wiring, and making knife rests. No digging was possible owing to the hard ground.	
	7th		Quiet day – Lieut Donohue died of wounds received in Action	
	8th		The enemy very active especially with trench mortars. Battn HQ at Surrey Farm was shelled, receiving 5 direct hits. Lt Conaghan was wounded and died next day.	

9 Vol
8B

16.N.
3 sheets

Army Form C. 2118

Instructions regarding War Diaries and Intelligence Summaries are contained in F. S. Regs., Part II. and the Staff Manual respectively. Title Pages will be prepared in manuscript.

WAR DIARY
or
INTELLIGENCE SUMMARY
(Erase heading not required.)

Place	Date	Hour	Summary of Events and Information	Remarks and references to Appendices
Trenches	9th		The enemy again active with trench mortars especially about 6pm doing considerable damage to the trenches held by Alg who had 2 casualties	
	10th		The Battn relieved of the x1 Cheshires and came back into support at LEBIZET A & D companies holding the front line A on the left & D on the right	
	11th		Church Parade. 50 men were employed as carrying party for the Trench Mortar Battery	
	12th-16		The Battn furnished carrying parties for the front line	
Trenches.	16th		The Bn relieved 11th Cheshires,) A Coy on left, C Centre, B on right & D in Support at Hattons Redoubt. – Enemy being quiet.	
	17th		Enemy Artillery active – our Artillery were put on to working party – who were dispersed Shouting was heard opposite ESSEX FARM	
	18th		Patrol went out at 9pm – opposite Gap C – to ascertain if Enemy were working on their wire – This was thought to be the case. Rifles Grenades were turned on – Workers hastily	
	19th		As arranged – our Artillery were very active at 7 & 9pm – The Enemy retaliated with 77 mm & 4.2" shells on Long Avenue – C Gap & behind [illegible] House – also T.M's which fell short of our line –) Pigeons were observed flying East from R.E. FRELINGHIEN	9716

1875 Wt. W593/826 1,000,000 4/15 J.B.C. & A. A.D.S.S./Forms/C. 2118.

Instructions regarding War Diaries and Intelligence Summaries are contained in F. S. Regs., Part II. and the Staff Manual respectively. Title Pages will be prepared in manuscript.

WAR DIARY
or
INTELLIGENCE SUMMARY
(Erase heading not required.)

Army Form C. 2118

Place	Date	Hour	Summary of Events and Information	Remarks and references to Appendices
Trenches	19th		During our Artillery activity 1 Red light & 1 Green rocket sent up from FRELINGHIEN.	
	20th		Between 4 & 4.30. Enemy shelled vicinity of C 16a 88 with field gun – afterwards range was shortened – & 3 shells fell round CARTERS FARM. Our Right Coy supports & around BARKENHAM HOUSE was shelled between 12.30 & 1 pm with field guns from SE. – Patrol went out to ascertain if Enemy was attempting to repair gaps made in Enemy wire by our Artillery – nothing was observed & Rifle fire was kept on gaps during the night	
	21st		Enemy sniping from opposite LE TOUQUET has increased – Enemy working party observed opposite C10 b 15.65. L.G. fire opened. – Sound of water pumped from trench opposite ESSEX CENTRAL heard at 11 pm & 3 am – Enemy has thrown many tins into NO MANS LAND between C4d 2.4 & C4c 9.8. – Heavy mist – Capt E. S. Philips died of wounds received in Action	
	22nd		Battn was relieved by New Zealand Bn & moved to LE BIZET	
	23rd		Working parties furnished for work on BARKENHAM AVENUE	
	24th		As yesterday.	
	25th		Battn moved to NIEPPE	
EECKE	26th		Battn marched with Bde. to EECKE	
	27th		Were engaged in cleaning billets & Equipment.	
	28th		Training under Coy arrangements – All specialists returned to Coys – Reorganisation of Platoons commenced – In afternoon – classes for Junior Officers & Reserve Teams –	97th [signature] [signature] Lt Col Comdg 1st Bn 8th Bde [illegible]

1875 Wt. W593/826 1,000,000 4/15 J.B.C. & A. A.D.S.S./Forms/C. 2118.

Headquarters,

75th. Infantry Brigade.

Herewith War Diary of the Battalion under my Command for the month of March, 1917.

C. E. Bond ....Lieutenant-Colonel,

1-4-17. Commanding 8th. Bn. Border Regiment.

Instructions regarding War Diaries and Intelligence Summaries are contained in F. S. Regs., Part II. and the Staff Manual respectively. Title Pages will be prepared in manuscript.

WAR DIARY
or
INTELLIGENCE SUMMARY
(Erase heading not required.)

Army Form C. 2118

8 Border Rgt

Vol 18

Place	Date	Hour	Summary of Events and Information	Remarks and references to Appendices
EECKE	Mch. 1st		Companies continue training under new organisation. In afternoon – Officers Classes of Instruction for Junior Officers in Lewis Gun – also for NCO's & men in Lewis Guns, Bombing – Signalling & Stretcher Bearers	
	2nd		2 Coys fired on Bertenacre Musketry Range – Coy training in morning – Bn Route march via FLETRE, THIEUSHOEK in afternoon. – Cold & misty weather –	
	3rd		Coy drill & training of ~~Specialists~~ Lewis Gunners &c in morning – Demonstration of Smoke Bombs & Gas Attack in afternoon – 3 Coys passed through Barrage of smoke & Gas & 4th Coy on morning of 4th. Lecture by C.O. to Officers & NCO's – on Advance Guards.	
	4th		Church Parade – & Recreational training – also Inter platoon football matches begun. OC – O/2nd in Com. & Adj. on Staff Ride – O.C. Coys rode in afternoon to reconnoitre ground for next day's practise Attack –	
	5th		Owing to high wind & much snow – Attack scheme postponed. – Bn Route march via STEENVORDE – & practise of small attack	
EBBLINGHEM	6th		Bn ~~marched~~ moved to EBBLINGHEM & billeted there for night – 11 miles	
NORTBÉCOURT	7th		Bn marched to NORTBÉCOURT – 16 miles – where billets had been arranged – Transport – with personnel billeted at LA WATTINE.	
	8th		Day spent cleaning up – inspections of [illegible] & Kits	
	9th		Firing on Range of 2nd Army Musketry School abandoned owing to snow & high wind – Coy training in Billets – Lecture to Officers by Capt Wilkinson – on Interior Economy	17. N. 4 sheets

1875 Wt. W593/826 1,000,000 4/15 J.B.C. & A. A.D.S.S./Forms/C. 2118.

Army Form C. 2118

Instructions regarding War Diaries and Intelligence Summaries are contained in F. S. Regs., Part II. and the Staff Manual respectively. Title Pages will be prepared in manuscript.

WAR DIARY
or
INTELLIGENCE SUMMARY

(Erase heading not required.)

Place	Date	Hour	Summary of Events and Information	Remarks and references to Appendices
	March 1917			
NORTBÉCOURT	10th		Bn fired on Musketry Range "B" – 32 Targets – firing practice, 13, 14 & 19, the same as Musketry School on the other 32 Targets – Coys not firing – training under Coy arrangements – on Miniature Range – PT & BF – Army Cdr. [illegible] firing – afterwards G.O.C. Division [illegible] firing behind cover – a waste of time.	
	11th		Lecture to Officers & NCO's by M.O. – on First Aid – Voluntary Church Service in afternoon – Baths under Coy arrangements in billets – Football match between Bn & 2nd Army School – Score – Borders 8 – A S 0. C.O. – on Staff Ride with 75th Bde – having left afternoon of 10th –	
	12th		Bn fired on Musketry Range – 14, 15, 16 & 17 practices – 80 men of B Coy to baths at HOULLE – (Musketry School baths)	
	13th		Bn Route march via LA WATTINE – MORINGHEM – INGLINGHEM – thence Practice Attack to windmill at CHISLINGHEM – returning 3 pm. 40 men baths at HOULLE – Weather raw & misty in morning, afterwards warm & sunny –	
	14th		Bn fired on Musketry Range practices 21, 22 & 23 – morning wet & misty – clear till 4 – then dull. G.O.C. Bde visited Billets –	
	15th		Bn under Coy arrangements – Night marching by Compass for Officers – Weather – very fine – Football match with R.F.C. – postponed –	
	16th		Bn fired on Musketry Range practice 23, 24 & 25 – the 2 latter being at 200 yds with Box Respirators	
	17th		Bn drill 9–10.15 am – afterwards Coy arrangements – Usual L.G. classes – Cross Country Race – 8th Borders v Musketry School (15 men per team) 8th Borders won – 16 men out of first 17 home – Weather – very fine – Strong wind	
	18th		Church Parade – Staff Ride from ACQUIN for Co, 2nd in C. & Adj – Afternoon – Musketry Field Practice – Day fine	
	19th		Coy training – In afternoon – preparation for marching off next day – Football Match against Musketry School detachment – Borders won 3 goals to 1 – Boxing Match Tournament in Evening – Col Bond to hospital with Rubella (German measles)	
ACQUIN	20th		March to ACQUIN – Afternoon – high wind & sleet	
EBBLINGHEM	21st		March to EBBLINGHEM – Cold & sleet	
BORRE	22nd		March to BORRE – Inspected on march by Lt Gen GODLEY – 2nd Anzac Corps – Cold & slight snow.	
"	23rd		Inspection & Coy training	
	24th		March to OUTTERSTEENE	
	25th		Church Parade in morning – L.G. & Bombing Classes in afternoon	
	26th		Coy training & Classes in L. Guns, Bombing etc, Officers Classes – Lecture by L.G. Officer to Officers & NCO's	

1875 Wt. W593/826 1,000,000 4/15 J.B.C. & A. A.D.S.S./Forms/C. 2118.

Army Form C. 2118

WAR DIARY
or
INTELLIGENCE SUMMARY
(Erase heading not required.)

Instructions regarding War Diaries and Intelligence Summaries are contained in F. S. Regs., Part II. and the Staff Manual respectively. Title Pages will be prepared in manuscript.

Place	Date	Hour	Summary of Events and Information	Remarks and references to Appendices
	March 1917			
OUTTERSTEENE	27		Bn inspected by Gen Sir H Plumer 2nd Army Commander. Coy training & specialist classes – Lecture by Capt Dawson on Reconnaissance – Day – [illegible]	
	28.		Coy training – Lecture by Bombing Officer – & lecture to men by M.O. – Usual classes – Showery. Capt Coxon reported – Brigade scheme for Adjts, Coy Cmdrs, Signal Officer & Bn Signallers	
	29.		Coy training – Lecture by T M B Officer – 1st Round of Football Match A v C Coy for Brigade Cup (A Coy won – 5-0). Bayonet fighting instruction by Bde Staff Sgt. Col Bond returned	
	30.		Route March via FLETRE to 1 Kilometre S of GODWAERSVELDE – A Coy beat Brigade 5-0 – B v D – Tie 1 Goal each	
	31.		Coy practise attack over flagged course at OUTTERSTEENE. B Coy beat D – 3-1.	

J. S. Wilkinson Capt
8 Border Regt

1875 Wt. W593/826 1,000,000 4/15 J.B.C. & A. A.D.S.S./Forms/C. 2118.

Instructions regarding War Diaries and Intelligence Summaries are contained in F. S. Regs., Part II. and the Staff Manual respectively. Title Pages will be prepared in manuscript.

Army Form C. 2118

WAR DIARY
or
INTELLIGENCE SUMMARY
(Erase heading not required.)

8 Border Regt

Vol 19

Place	Date	Hour	Summary of Events and Information	Remarks and references to Appendices
	April 1917			
OUTTERSTEENE	Apl 1.		[illegible] - Coy inspections.	
"	Apl 2		Inter platoon Bombing Competitions - C Coy won 26 pts, B Coy 19, A & D 11 pts - 2nd S Lancs Sports in afternoon - Brigadier & Bde Major dined at Bn HQrs	
	" 3.		C.O. & O.C. Coys, [illegible] officers to trenches at WULVERGHEM. Usual Coy training	
NEUVE EGLISE	4		Bn moved to NEUVE EGLISE area - 2nd in Com. & Adjutant to trenches	
WULVERGHEM	5.		Bn relieves 1st OTAGO N.Z. Bde - D Coy on left, C Coy on R - A left Support, B right Support - A Coy - SCOTLAND Fm, GALWAY Dugouts, DESTROYED WINDMILL - B Coy - FORRES TERRACE	
"			A & B supplied working parties for front line - Heavy Artillery bombardment, at 8.30 pm - Enemy retaliated - 3 casualties D Coy, 2 N.Z. T.M. Battery killed & 1 R.E.	
	6.		A & B working parties - 40 each in morning & night - Day - cold & wet - Fairly quiet day	
	7		A & B working parties, 20 morning, 20 afternoon & 40 night - Day very clear. T.M. active in morning on left - 5 pm heavy enemy artillery [illegible] on left - [illegible] retaliated -	
	8		Working parties as usual - Little activity - Weather very fine	
	9.		A relieved D, B relieved C in line. Relief completed by 6.30 am - Col Bird left to command 7th Bde temporarily - Unsettled weather - R.I.R. Officers went round trenches	
	10		Blizzard in morning - Usual working parties - Day - quiet	
	10/11		~~Usual working parties~~ - Patrol 10/11th reported movement opposite bombing post N 36/7 - ~~[illegible]~~ -	
	11.		Cold wild weather with Snow - No night working parties or patrols	
	12		Usual working parties - Enemy active with Minenwerfer opposite Bombing Block N/36.7. Night quiet - Day - fine.	
	13.		Bn relieved by 2nd R. I.R. - G.O.C. Div. & Bde through front line	
STEENT-JE	14		Arrived in billets - 2 am - Bn rested & cleaned up	
	15		Church Parade - Officers reconnoitred Attack Course at BAILLEUL. Wet - & attack in afternoon postponed	
	Mon 16.		Coy training in morning. Also Baths - Attack over Course in afternoon - Training for Sports - C Coy 10 Pl. chosen to represent Bn.	
	Tu 17.		Wet morning - Sports postponed - Fine afternoon - Working parties supplied 360 men	Wild & wet day
	W 18		Heavy snow - Sports Cancelled - Working parties 360 men - ~~[illegible]~~	
	Th 19		O.C. Coys watched attack by 11th Cheshires - Preparing for move in morning - Day - wet & cold -	
PONT DE NIEPPE	F 20		Cleaning up billets - Bn took over billets from 2nd S. Lancs Regt. Day - fine -	
	S 21		Working parties supplied all day - 1 man from C Coy killed, 1 wounded returning near Chapelle Rompue - Day - fine & warm	
	Sun 22.		Working parties as usual - Church Parade - Day - fine & warm.	
	23.		Usual working parties (4 Coys) - Cable laying - Soyer Farm, & moving Stores - Bn Concert at night, with Divisional Orchestra - attended by Brigadier & Staff - 2nd Lt Jones 3rd Worcesters - attached for duty -	

1875 Wt. W593/826 1,000,000 4/15 J.B.C. & A. A.D.S.S./Forms/C. 2118.

18. N.
2 sheets

Instructions regarding War Diaries and Intelligence Summaries are contained in F. S. Regs., Part II. and the Staff Manual respectively. Title Pages will be prepared in manuscript.

WAR DIARY
or
INTELLIGENCE SUMMARY
(Erase heading not required.)

Army Form C. 2118

Place	Date	Hour	Summary of Events and Information	Remarks and references to Appendices
	April 1917			
PONT DE NIEPPE	Th 24		Usual working parties. Major Outt Birt & 2nd Lieut F. W. Haswell (4th Border T.F.) reported for duty. Day fine. Inspected all Lewis Guns	
	W 25		do - 1 LG section sent to TOOL HOUSE to assist Bn in line. Night Compass march for Officers. Day warm & fine.	
	Th 26		do. and LG and Bombing classes. Enemy shelled Bridge over River Lys during the day. Slight damage. Day cloudy - clearing up toward dark.	
	F 27		do & LG & Bombing classes. Night working parties cancelled. Day cloudy. Lecture to ~~War~~ Officers & NCOs in afternoon by Major Birt. & Night marching by Compass for Officers	
	S 28		do & LG & Bombing classes. Day cloudy & warm. Boxing tournament in evening.	
Erquinghem	29		Cleaned up Billets. Marched to Erquinghem & took over Billets in Laundry from Australians in afternoon, fine & warm	
	M 30		Cleaning up. Physical drill. Baths at Laundry morning. Afternoon marched with Brigade to Billets near Outersteene. Day fine & warm. Church Parade.	
Outersteene	May 1917 1st			

J. S. Wilkinson Major
8 Border Regt
30.4.17

1875 Wt. W593/826 1,000,000 4/15 J.B.C. & A. A.D.S.S./Forms/C. 2118.

Instructions regarding War Diaries and Intelligence Summaries are contained in F. S. Regs., Part II. and the Staff Manual respectively. Title Pages will be prepared in manuscript.

WAR DIARY
or
~~INTELLIGENCE SUMMARY~~
(Erase heading not required.)

Army Form C. 2118

8 Border Rgt
Vol 20

19.N
2 sheets

Place	Date 1917	Hour	Summary of Events and Information	Remarks and references to Appendices
OUTTERSTEENE	May 1.		Col Bond arrived from leave – also Capt Turner. RAMC – 2nd Lieut DREW (11th Border) reported for duty – Brigade Conference 10 am – 1 officer Platoon HQrs & 1 Section Riflemen reported to Brigade for Brigade Platoon – Coy training – Day very fine & warm.	
	2		Coy training – Bde signalling scheme in afternoon – attended by O.C.'s, Adjt & Sig officers – also Border signallers – Beautiful day.	
	3.		do – 11 Cheshire v 8th Lancs – draw 1 goal each – Conference of OC Coys & CSM – to draw up Bn sports programme. do.	
	4		do – Coys visited by Brigadier, DA QMG, & Expert from Army S. of Cookery – Coy Bombing Contest, B & C, Brown – held arranged for sports – do.	
	5		do Bn sports in afternoon (from Rations turned over) – Bde Cross Country Race 11th Cheshire 1st, 8th Border 2nd. Open air concert abruptly – Day fine – cold at night	
	6.		Church Service in barn at HQrs. Day fine – OC Coys reconnoitred ground for practice attack tomorrow. Fine	
	7.		Brigade Practice attack over Mont de Lille training ground. Afternoon – Officers reconnoitred ground for night Compass march. Day fine	
	8.		Bde Practice attack postponed – Coys attack over same area – Officers night compass march. Day – cloudy & wet in morning – fine later	
	9.		Coy training – 24 men paraded before A.D.M.S.	
STEENT-JE	10		do Major Wilkinson, Company Cdrs & QMr to Cookery School Hazebrouck for instruction. In afternoon Battalion moved to Billets in Steent-je area. Photo's taken. Warm	
	11		Coy training. Colonel Bond to Brigade & Major Wilkinson on Leave. Fine & warm. Major Birt Commanding. Capt Smith to "A" Coy	
	12.		Battalion to Mont de Lille training ground. Practice attack. C. Coy 50 men Strazeele area Working Party. Warm	
	13		"C" & "D" Coys away at 5 am. to Neuve Eglise – detached for several days Working Party. Church parade. Cricket Match "A" versus "B" Coy in afternoon. – Won by B Coy. 76 runs to 28. Capt Dawson to Cookery School for days instruction. Thunderstorm	
	14.		"A" & "B" Coys to Mont de Lille training ground for Company training & firing exercises. Boxing Contest evening. Cloudy & little rain in afternoon.	
LA CRECHE	15		"A" & "B" Coys & Headquarters moved to Billets & Bivouacs at La Creche. "C" & "D" remaining at Neuve Eglise. Cloudy & cool.	
	16		"A" & "B" Coys to Mont de Lille training ground for Company training in Attack & firing exercises. 200 men to DE KENNEBAC Siding to unload Munitions. Working all night. Cool day. Very wet night	
	17		Wet. Only a few men available for training. Major Birt, Capts Coxon, Lay, Stewart & Dawson to view Model Enemy trenches at LOCRE. 200 men to DeKENNEBAK Siding to unload munitions. Away all night.	
	18		Wet Only a few men available for training. C & D Coys still at Neuve Eglise	
	19		"A" & "B" Coys provided working party 200 men for unloading at DEKENNEBAK Siding. C & D at NEUVE EGLISE	
	20		Fine. "A" & "B" Coys provided working party 200 men at DEKENNEBAK. Church parade at 10.30am. CO & Major Birt to C & D Coys in afternoon. C.O. returned from Brigade	
	21		Fine C & D Coys at NEUVE EGLISE. A & B resting & Bathing. Officers & NCOs to MONT DE LILLE to watch attack by 8th S Lancs Brigade Boxing Competitions in evening. All Shields taken in 10 hd Contest by Pte Newbiggan 11 Cheshire	

Army Form C. 2118

Instructions regarding War Diaries and Intelligence Summaries are contained in F. S. Regs., Part II. and the Staff Manual respectively. Title Pages will be prepared in manuscript.

WAR DIARY
or
INTELLIGENCE SUMMARY
(Erase heading not required.)

Place	1917 Date May	Hour	Summary of Events and Information	Remarks and references to Appendices
LA CRECHE	T 22		Close & muggy with little rain. C+D Coys still at NEUVE EGLISE. A+B Coys to MONT DE LILLE for practice attack in conjunction with XI Chesh. Divisional Cdr present. Attack was done well. Coy training in morning.	
	W 23		Cool. A+B Coys doing Company training. LG Sections firing on small range at STEENWERCK. C+D Coys at NEUVE EGLISE. Officers & NCOs to watch practice attack by 8th & 2nd S Lancs on MONT DE LILLE in afternoon. Corps, Divisional & Brigade Cdrs present. Capt W.O. LAY came down to HQ on way to take post as Staff Capt. 70th Brigade. 200 men to DEKENNEBAK Siding unloading munitions. Away all night.	
	Th 24		Fine. C+D Coys returned from Neuve Eglise area - relieved by 2 Coys 8th S Lancs. Company training. 80 men A Coy & to DEKENNEBAK Siding as working party at night.	
	F 25		Warm. Coy training in morning & D Coy to Baths. In afternoon the Battalion did a practice attack on MONT DE LILLE training ground.	
	S 26		Battalion took part in Brigade exercise on MONT DE LILLE with XI Chesh. in morning. Working party of 80 men from B Coy to DEKENNEBAK Siding. Back 11 pm. Nos 1.2.3 Lewis Gun teams on Range & Rifle Grenadiers on Bombing pit. Warm. Bathing.	
	S 27		Very Warm. East wind. Church parade 9.30 am. Lewis Gun 1.2 & 3's on Range & Rifle Grenadiers on Bombing pit. Bathing.	
	M 28		Very Warm. A.B.C & D Coys to MONT DE LILLE training area for attack practice under Brigade arrangements. Concert in evening - good. Major Birt & Mr Anderson up to see trenches.	
RAVELSBURG	T 29		Cool & cloudy. Battalion marched to Ravelsburg in morning - tents & bivouacs. Cross Country run - Borders beaten by XI Cheshire. Recreation in afternoon.	
	W 30		Warm. A+B Coys Company training - Musketry & Bayonets - C+D Coys supplied 200 men working party SOUVENIR FARM. Shell burst as C Coy were going down NEUVE EGLISE Road killing 4 & wounding 6 men. Lewis Gun teams on range. Lt Col Bond (O.C.) received notice of his appointment to Command of 51st Brigade.	
	Th 31		Fine. A+B Coys on fatigues. C+D Coys doing Company training. Lewis Gun teams on Range. "B" teams of Battalion under Major Wilkinson left for Morbecque	

C.W.H. Birt Major
7c 8th Bn Border Regt

1875 Wt. W593/826 1,000,000 4/15 J.B.C. & A. A.D.S.S./Forms/C. 2118

Instructions regarding War Diaries and Intelligence Summaries are contained in F. S. Regs., Part II. and the Staff Manual respectively. Title Pages will be prepared in manuscript.

WAR DIARY
or
INTELLIGENCE SUMMARY
(Erase heading not required.)

Army Form C. 2118

8th Gordon Regt 75/75

Vol 21

Place	Date 1917	Hour	Summary of Events and Information	Remarks and references to Appendices
RAVELSBERG	June 1		Fine. C+D Coys provided working parties of 100 men each. A+B Coys doing Company training. Lewis Gun teams on Range. Brigadier General C.E. BOND. CMG.-DSO. left the Battalion to take over 51st Brigade.	
	2		Fine. A+B Coys provided working parties of 100 men each. C+D Coys did Company training. Lewis Gun teams on Range at Crucifix Corner. Church parades in evening - 7 oclock.	
PIONEER CAMP NEUVE EGLISE	S 3		Fine. A+B Coys left RAVELSBURG CAMP at 5am to take over DURHAM TRENCHES from 1st Wilts. C+D moved out at 6.30am to take over Bivouacs at PIONEER Camp from remaining Coys of 1st Wilts. C+D finding working parties for RE Coys. Parties visited Model trenches CONNAUGHT ROAD. 'B' Coy 2 casualties wounded.	
	M 4		Fine + warm. A+B Coys in Durham Trench. - B Coy 1 Casualty - wounded. C+D Coys doing R E work.	
	T 5		Warm. A+B Coys in Durham Trench. C+D provided working parties for Engineers. Heavy Bombardment all night.	
	W 6		Warm. East Wind. C+D relieved A+B Coys in Durham Line early this morning. B Coy had 2 casualties during its stay in the Durham trench. The Battalion in assembly trenches Newcastle Trench soon after midnight preparatory to attacking in the morning. Stores, tools re issued at Pioneer Camp.	
MESSINES RIDGE	Th 7		Warm. Attack on MESSINES RIDGE began at 3.10 am. Battalion left Assembly trench (Newcastle) at 7am to take part. C on left, D on right. A+B in Support respectively. Provisional task - consolidation of Black Line - just East of MESSINES - WYTSCHAETE Road, but had to keep clear several pockets of enemy left by advancing troops. Reached Black Line about 8.30 am + began Consolidation, Also dug 2 CTs [illegible] from October Support Trench - one on right + one of left of our position. 2nd S Lancs moved the front at night. Enemy shelled very heavily at intervals all the day + night. 2/Lt G Healy killed during Advance + 2/Lt Bott + 2/Lt Johnson wounded. Sent 4 platoons forward to Support 9th Cheshires on O.P. Line.	
	F 8		Warm. Consolidation proceeding. Shelled at intervals all day. Heavy shelling at night - reported Counter attack at night on 4th Australian Division in front. Relieved about Midnight by 2 Companies of 1st N[?]. Total Casualties 1 Officer Killed, 2 Wounded. 13 O.R. Killed, 65 wounded.	
NEUVE EGLISE	S 9		Warm. Battalion in Brigade Camp resting + refitting. Major General Bainbridge visited Camp.	
	S 10		Fine. In Camp resting + refitting. Church parade 11 am	

1875 Wt. W593/826 1,000,000 4/15 J.B.C. & A. A.D.S.S./Forms/C. 2118.

20. N.
2 sheets

Instr[illegible]garding War Diaries and Intelligence Summaries are contained in F. S. Regs., Part II. and the Staff Manual respectively. Title Pages will be prepared in manuscript.

WAR DIARY
or
INTELLIGENCE SUMMARY
(Erase heading not required.)

Army Form C. 2118

Place	1917 Date	Hour	Summary of Events and Information	Remarks and references to Appendices
NEUVE EGLISE	June M. 11		Cool & cloudy. Still in Camp. Corps Commander II ANZAC CORPS visited Camp in morning & personally thanked the whole Brigade for splendid work done in the attack on MESSINES RIDGE. Battalion did little Company drill. Also Baths allotted.	
do	T. 12		Cool & showery. Bn moved up to trenches – Messines sector – Bn Transport at KANDAHAR Camp.	
MESSINES	W 13		Fine – Artillery bombardment – 2/Lt W.H. Anderson killed on patrol into Mag? Bert	
	Th 14		Bn attacked from Assembly position in new Switch trench – A, B & D from R to L with C Coy in support – & attacked at. with objective FERME de la CROIX – V 5 d 12 40 – LES QUATRE ROIS CABt – GAPAARD – DECONINCK FARM – which was successfully accomplished) 2Lt W.A. BELL killed – Major BIRT, Captns STEWART & DAWSON wounded – the 2 former joined Bn team & Capt DAWSON was evacuated	
	FR. 15.		Fine – Bn continued consolidation & was relieved by XI CHESHIRES & moved into support.	
	SAT 16		Fine – Working parties furnished.	
DE KENNEBEK	SUN 17		Fine – Bn moved out to Camp at DE KENNEBEK siding.	
	MON 18		Fine – Bn refitted & rested.	
	TUE 19.		Fine – Parades under Coy arrangement. Lt Col. BIRT on short leave.	
	WED. 20		Cloudy – Bn route march – Recreational training	
	Th 21		Wet – Route march cancelled – Coy training	
	Fr. 22		Fine – Coy training – various events for the Coy Cup run off	
SEC BOIS	23		Bn moved to SEC BOIS leaving 9.50 pm Fine	
MERVILLE	24		Bn moved to MERVILLE at 10.45 pm – Fine	
ST HILAIRE	25		Bn moved to ST HILAIRE leaving 10.40 pm Wet	
ERNY ST JULIEN	26		" – ERNY ST JULIEN – leaving 11.20 – Fine	
"	27		Billets. Attempt made to clean filthy billets – Wet in afternoon	
"	28		Coy training – Lt Gen JACOBS Corps Cmdr addressed officers of 75 Bde at BOMY	
"	29		Fine. Coy training. Major Wilkinson left for Aldershot course	
"	30		Wet. Coy. training. Lecture in evening by Col. Birt to N.C.Os & Officers.	

[illegible] Capt & Adjt.
[illegible] Border Regt.

1875 Wt. W593/826 1,000,000 4/15 J.B.C. & A. A.D.S.S./Forms/C. 2118.

Instructions regarding War Diaries and Intelligence Summaries are contained in F. S. Regs., Part II. and the Staff Manual respectively. Title Pages will be prepared in manuscript.

WAR DIARY
or
~~INTELLIGENCE~~ SUMMARY
(Erase heading not required.)

Army Form C. 2118

Vol 22

Place	Date 1917 July	Hour	Summary of Events and Information	Remarks and references to Appendices
ERNY ST JULIEN	S 1		Threatening. Church parade on Bn. parade ground with 8th S.Lancs + Bde HQrs + 76th F.A. Football match on Battalion parade ground 8th Borders V XI Cheshires. Won by Borders 5 goals to 1.	
	M 2		Beautiful day. Battn (less LG teams) to Long Range near BOMY for Rifle shooting. LG teams on Miniature Range at ERNY St JULIEN.	
	T 3		Warm. Battn doing Individual training. LG teams on Miniature Range. C.O. Adjt + Coy Cdrs to CUHEM for Brigade Staff Ride	
	W 4		Very wet. Battn marched to CUHEM for Bde practice Attack. Attack cancelled owing to rain. Returned to Billets + carried on with Individual training – Musketry + Bayonet fighting.	
	T 5		Fine. Brigade practice attack – from CUHEM – BOMY Road. Battalion attacked thro ERNY ST JULIEN to the high ground North West of village. Attack repeated in afternoon. Ceremonial Parade in front of Church for presentation of Medal Ribbons by G.O.C. Brigade, + Guard mounting. Football Battn team played 77th F. Ambulance on our ground + won 3 goals to 1. LG teams on Miniature Range.	
	F 6		Beautiful day. Battalion ceremonial parade in morning. Coys on Long Range afternoon. LG teams + classes on Miniature Range.	
	S 7		Fine. Bathing parties to BOMY morning. Battalion practice attack in afternoon. LG teams ~~[illegible]~~ on range + new draft at Bombing pits.	
STEENBECQUE	S 8		Very wet overnight – cloudy all day. Battalion moved in Buses + Lorries to STEENBECQUE (billets)	
WINNIPEG CAMP OUDERDOM	M 9		Cloudy + cold. Battalion moved with rest of Brigade OUDERDOM area – in huts at WINNIPEG Camp. (per Buses + Lorries)	
	T 10		Fine. Company parades in morning. Resting + cleaning up afternoon. Party of 502 all ranks under Capt Coxon moved on in Lorries at night to SWAN CHATEAU. New drafts paraded under RSM for drill. Capt Read (8th S.Lancs) arrived to take over Second in Command temporarily.	
	W 11		Fine. Cleaning up. Drafts paraded under RSM + new LG classes (6 per Coy) started under Lt Otway. Signallers paraded under 2/Lt Clodd.	
	Th. 12		Fine. Range finding class (2 per Coy) started under 2/Lt Laycock. Work of other instructional classes continued. Working parties supplied from SWAN CHATEAU for road making + cable laying. Capt. Stewart returned from leave.	H.N. [illegible]

1875 Wt. W593/826 1,000,000 4/15 J.B.C. & A. A.D.S.S./Forms/C. 2118.

Army Form C. 2118

Instructions regarding War Diaries and Intelligence Summaries are contained in F. S. Regs., Part II. and the Staff Manual respectively. Title Pages will be prepared in manuscript.

WAR DIARY
or
~~INTELLIGENCE SUMMARY~~
(Erase heading not required.)

Place	Date	Hour	Summary of Events and Information	Remarks and references to Appendices
WINNIPEG CAMP OUDERDOM	1917 July F 13		Fine day, rain during night. Fourteen of draft sent to SWAN CHATEAU to take place of men withdrawn to attend instructional classes. Work of parties during night hindered by hostile shelling. Casualties 7 killed 17 wounded.	
	Sat. 14		Close during day, thunderstorms at night. Work of instructional classes continued. Scouts also taken by 2/Lt. Laycock in range finding. Casualties from working party 1 killed 7 wounded.	
	S. 15		Fine. Church parades at WINNIPEG CAMP and SWAN CHATEAU. Men attending Lewis Gun Classes returned to SWAN CHATEAU to strengthen working party. (6 per Coy.)	
	M 16		Fine. Remainder of draft (totalling 38) and range finding class (8 men) returned to SWAN CHATEAU to strengthen working party whose numbers were depleted owing to sickness caused by lachrymatory gas. 2/Lt. J. Duggan returned from leave.	
	T. 17		Fine. Trained signallers only available for instruction. Casualties among working party 5 wounded.	
	W. 18		Showery. During the morning demonstration given to all available men of the use of the Yukon Pack. Only one working party of 270 men required from today at SWAN CHATEAU. Remainder to be relieved by 8th South Lancs. 2/Lt. H. MacTavish returned from Rest Camp. 2/Lt. John Davidson, 2/Lt. James Silva Kamester, 2/Lt. Robert Smith } These officers reported to-day from the Base and were taken on the strength of the Batt.	

1875 Wt. W593/826 1,000,000 4/15 J.B.C. & A. A.D.S.S./Forms/C. 2118.

Instructions regarding War Diaries and Intelligence Summaries are contained in F. S. Regs., Part II. and the Staff Manual respectively. Title Pages will be prepared in manuscript.

WAR DIARY

or

~~INTELLIGENCE SUMMARY~~

(Erase heading not required.)

Army Form C. 2118

Place	Date 1917 July	Hour	Summary of Events and Information	Remarks and references to Appendices
WINNIPEG CAMP OUDERDOM	Th. 19		Fine. Day spent by men returned from SWAN CHATEAU in cleaning equipment and ammunition. Men paraded for inspection at 3 p.m. 20 men returned to SWAN CHATEAU to make strength of working party there 270, exclusive of sergeants stretcher bearers and duty men. Casualties on working party 4 wounded. 100 men detailed from Camp for work under Lt. Birnie. Returned 3 a.m.	
	F. 20		Fine. 33 men sent to reinforce detachment at SWAN CHATEAU. Deficiency caused by casualties & sickness. Classes of instruction continued. Working parties totalling 67 detailed from Camp for work during night. Casualties nil.	
	Sat. 21		Fine. Work of instructional classes continued. Working parties supplied as on previous day. Their work was considerably interfered with through gas. Casualties 2 killed 4 wounded 24 gassed.	
	S. 22		Fine. Church parades at WINNIPEG CAMP and SWAN CHATEAU. Working parties supplied from both the above places for night work (270 and 76 respectively). Remainder of Battalion moved at 9-45 p.m. to RENINGHELST STAGING AREA 'A'. Working parties on completion of tasks were conveyed by motor lorries to the above Camp.	
RENINGHELST STAGING AREA 'A'	M. 23		Fine. Day spent by men in cleaning equipment. Also kit inspection & reorganisation throughout Battalion.	
	T. 24		Fine. Programme of training as follows: 7 a.m. – 7-30. Physical training 9-15 – 9-45 Battalion parade 9-45 – 12-30 Classes of instruction & Coy. training 2 p.m. to 4 p.m. Classes of instruction & recreational training. A party of 50 men & 5 officers assembled at Brigade Headquarters to hear an address given by the Archbishop of York.	

1875 Wt. W593/826 1,000,000 4/15 J.B.C. & A. A.D.S.S./Forms/C. 2118.

Instructions regarding War Diaries and Intelligence Summaries are contained in F. S. Regs., Part II. and the Staff Manual respectively. Title Pages will be prepared in manuscript.

WAR DIARY
or
~~INTELLIGENCE SUMMARY~~
(Erase heading not required.)

Army Form C. 2118

Place	Date	Hour	Summary of Events and Information	Remarks and references to Appendices
RENINGHELST STAGING AREA 'A'	W 25th		Fine. Physical training 7a.m – 7-30. Battn parade 9-15 to 9-45 a.m. 9-45 – 12-30 Special Instruction Classes. Remainder Musketry & bayonet fighting. The Brigade assembled at 2-45p.m on 8th South Lancs parade ground & were addressed by the Divisional General.	
	T. 26		Fine. Physical training 7-7-30. Battn parade 9-15 – 9-45. Specialist classes 9-45-12-30. Lewis Gun classes continued 2 – 4p.m. During afternoon Inter-Company Football & Tug of war competitions.	
	F. 27.		Fine. Training as on previous day. Army Commander – Gen. Gough visited ~~our~~ camp at 1-10p.m. He was accompanied by the Brig. Gen. & Divnl General. During the afternoon the Commanding Officer demonstrated use of Yukon Pack to the Carrying Platoons.	
	Sat. 28		Fine. Training programme continued. Battn football team played 15th Cheshires in semifinal Divnl Competition and lost 1 – 0. Lt. Blodd gave demonstration of use of Yukon Pack to Battns of 7th Brigade. No classes during afternoon.	
	S. 29.		Heavy thunderstorms during morning. Church parade at 11-30 a.m. Men rested during remainder of day.	
	M. 30.		Showery. Battalion paraded during morning in fighting order for inspection. ~~A draft of~~ A draft of men joined the battalion at 6p.m. – 1 N.C.O. & 55 men –. At 2p.m. B Team (including C.S.Ms.) marched to OUDEZEELE. At 7-30p.m. 'T' Team under Capt. Reade marched to Transport Lines. The remainder of Battalion left camp at 9-30p.m. & marched to position of assembly immediately SOUTH of BELGIAN CHATEAU.	

1875 Wt. W593/826 1,000,000 4/15 J.B.C. & A. A.D.S.S./Forms/C. 2118.

Instructions regarding War Diaries and Intelligence Summaries are contained in F. S. Regs., Part II. and the Staff Manual respectively. Title pages will be prepared in manuscript.

WAR DIARY
or
~~INTELLIGENCE SUMMARY.~~
(Erase heading not required.)

Army Form C. 2118.

Place	Date	Hour	Summary of Events and Information	Remarks and references to Appendices
BELGIAN CHATEAU AREA.	July 31.		Fine. Battalion moved from Assembly Area at 7.40 a.m. to position of readiness. During the night we took over the line gained by the 2nd West Yorks Regt – the 8th Division having attacked during the morning. Casualties 9 wounded including Lt. King wounded at duty.	

Army Form C. 2118.

Instructions regarding War Diaries and Intelligence Summaries are contained in F. S. Regs., Part II. and the Staff Manual respectively. Title pages will be prepared in manuscript.

WAR DIARY
or
~~INTELLIGENCE SUMMARY.~~
(Erase heading not required.)

8th Border Regt.

Vol 23

Place	Date	Hour	Summary of Events and Information	Remarks and references to Appendices
	1917			
BELLEWARDE FARM	August 1		At 1.30am Battalion was ordered from Mud Lane to take up position in close support of 23rd Bde who were holding BELLEWARDE RIDGE. At 4am the Bn was in position between BELLEWARDE LAKE and YPRES–ROULERS RAILWAY. C Coy (Capt KING) & D Coy (Capt DUGGAN) right & left front respectively A Coy (Capt SMITH) & B Coy (Lieut BIRNIE M.C.) in Support – Battalion HQ & Aid post at BELLEWARDE FARM. Rained heavily all day. Men suffered from exposure & cold. Enemy shelled the position fairly continuously. Two parties 40 men each sent forward at night to assist dig support trenches on West slope of WESTHOEK RIDGE	
	2		Still in position North of BELLEWARDE LAKE. Rained nearly all day. Warning received of probable counter attack on BLACK LINE (WESTHOEK RIDGE). Bn held in readiness to move forward to BELLEWARDE RIDGE and to counter attack if necessary. Shelled intermittently	
	3		Still in BELLEWARDE Position. Acting under orders G.O.C. Bde who visited us in the morning a party of 100 men under Capt J J Gemmel Smith was detailed to assist the XI CHESHIRES who were attacking next morning in order to push their forward posts out a couple of hundred yards. Owing to the continued rain the attack was postponed. Sec Lieut W.F.J. LAIT (D Coy) Killed in Action near LAKE FARM.	
	4		Still in BELLEWARDE Position. Weather finer but threatening.	
	5		Still in BELLEWARDE Position. Little rain. Ground in very muddy state. Movement difficult	
RAILWAY WOOD	6		Bn relieved early in morning by 1 Coy L.N. Lancs & 1 Coy Lanc. Fus. and moved back to Dug outs in RAILWAY WOOD	
	7		More rain. 2 Working parties of 110 men each provided for 74th Bde to carry [illegible]. At 10pm Bn moved forward. A & C Coys (Capts SMITH and KING resp.) to JACOB TRENCH – A on right. D Coy (Capt COXON M.C.) north of LAKE FARM. B Coy (Lt BIRNIE M.C.) IDIOT RESERVE. H.Q. & AID POST at BELLEWARDE FARM.	
BELLEWARDE	8		Bn ordered to be prepared to assist 74th Bde in projected attack. A Coy placed under orders Lt Col FINCH (13 Cheshires) to support his right flank South of WESTHOEK. D Coy brought into JACOB TRENCH to be vacated by A Coy, and B Coy sent down to RAILWAY WOOD to assist carrying parties. Aid post at BELLEWARDE FARM and Bn H.Q. at junction JACOB TRENCH and IDIOT DRIVE. All in position by 12 midnight 8/9th Aug. Rained heavily & enemy shelled very heavily	

CWHB

22. N.
3 sheets

T2134. Wt. W708–776. 500000. 4/15. Sir J. C. & S.

Instructions regarding War Diaries and Intelligence Summaries are contained in F. S. Regs., Part II. and the Staff Manual respectively. Title pages will be prepared in manuscript.

WAR DIARY
or
INTELLIGENCE SUMMARY.
(*Erase heading not required.*)

Army Form C. 2118.

Place	Date 1917	Hour	Summary of Events and Information	Remarks and references to Appendices
BELLEWARDE	Aug 9th		Attack postponed owing to unpropitious weather & by 6am the Bn was moved back to the position occupied by it 24 hours previously. At 11.30pm the Battalion was relieved by the 3rd WORCESTERS & moved back via MENIN GATE & BELGIAN BATTERY CORNER (where lorries were waiting) to WINNIPEG CAMP. Sec Lt R SMITH Died of wounds received in action while he was being relieved.	
WINNIPEG	10		Bn resting & refitting in Camp. "B" teams from Transport rejoined. Men bathed.	
	11		Warned to move back to line to relieve 2nd R Irish R. Lt Col BIRT went forward to arrange relief with 74th Bde. Bn moved by lorries to BELGIAN BATT CORNER thence marched via WARRINGTON ROAD and BIRR CROSS ROADS to position on WESTHOEK RIDGE. Owing to enemy barrage & heavy rain, & guides not being at appointed place relief much delayed. Ground very wet & boggy.	
WESTHOEK	12		Bn completed relief of 2nd Royal Irish Rifles by 3.30am & disposed as follows. A Coy (2/Lt HASWELL) J8 a 65.20 – B Coy (Capt Coxon M.C.) J8 a 50.40. C Coy (Capt KING) J8 a 60.65. D Coy (2/Lt CROOKSTON) J8 a 60.75 – all on eastern slope of WESTHOEK RIDGE. Aid post at SEIBEN HOUSE. Bn HQ J 7 d 80.90. Morning was fine but rain fell heavily in afternoon. Movement during day practically impossible. Position shelled very heavily especially at night. By 11.30pm the Battalion was relieved – the 2 right Coys by 3rd Lon[illegible] & 2 left Coys by XI Cheshires, & moved via BELGIAN BATTERY CORNER (where lorries were waiting) to DOMINION CAMP. Capt F J Gemmel-Smith Wounded.	
DOMINION CAMP	13		Bn all in Camp by 8am except for one or two stragglers. Transport & the B teams with Transport moved from forward transport lines (near BELGIAN CHATEAU) to DOMINION CAMP. The day spent in resting & cleaning up. Little rain.	
	14		Heavy rain during the day. Bn resting, cleaning up & refitting. Capt TURNER (M.O) sent down sick & Capt WELLS sent from 76 FA to relieve him. Capt READE rejoined his Battalion 8th Shanes[?]	
	15		Thunder showers. Battalion refitting. B teams rejoined & reinforcements from MILLAM. Capt Dove 2/Lts HOGG, OAKDEN, & LAY joined from Corps Reinforcement Camp. Brig Genl C E BOND (late C.O) paid the Battalion a visit.	

C.W.H.B.

T2134. Wt. W708—776. 500000. 4/15. Sir J. C. & S.

Instructions regarding War Diaries and Intelligence Summaries are contained in F. S. Regs., Part II. and the Staff Manual respectively. Title pages will be prepared in manuscript.

WAR DIARY
or
~~INTELLIGENCE SUMMARY.~~

(Erase heading not required.)

Army Form C. 2118.

Place	Date	Hour	Summary of Events and Information	Remarks and references to Appendices
	Aug[t]			
DOMINION CAMP	16		Received short notice to move up to Divisional Reserve. Left at 12 noon for SWAN CHATEAU – no casualties. Carrying parties (5 of 50) – for 8th Div[n], carrying to DUMP by BELLEWARDE RIDGE. Casualties – NIL.	
SWAN CH[au]	17		Relieved in evening by 17/Londons & marching to embussing point on OUDERDOM – FLAMERTIGHNE Rd.	
GODEWEARSVELDT	18		Arrived at Billets at 4 a.m. Major F.A. WILSON – 1st R. Dublin Fus. joined Bn for duty as 2nd in Command.	
-do-	19		Church pde & cleaning up.	
-do-	20		Brigade moved to STEENVORDE. AREA. Left at 9 a.m. – marched in Bn. Lieut. Col. C.W.H. BIRT. DSO. left Bn. for weeks rest at sea-side.	
STEENVORDE	21		General Inspection by C-in-C. Field Marshal SIR DOUGLAS HAIG. K.C.B. etc. Bn. did very well – Complimented by C. in C.	
-do-	22		General & Specialist Training in morning – Recreational Training in afternoon.	
-do-	23		-do- -do-	
-do-	24		-do- -do- Competition for BOND CUP completed – A Coy. winners.	
-do-	25		General & Specialist Training in morning – Recreational Training in afternoon. Lieut. Col. C.W.H. BIRT DSO rejoined Bn.	
~~-do-~~	~~25~~			
-do-	26		Church parade. C.O's Conference at Bde H.Q. (Short). Heavy rain at night.	
-do-	27		Heavy rain. Indoor classes. C.O's Tactical Exercise for Senior Officers.	
-do-	28		-do- -do-	
-do-	29		Bde Horse Show & Sports. Bn tied with 1/Cheshires for 1st place in Transport events & scored highest points in Athletic events.	
-do-	30		General & Specialist Training in morning – Final for Divisional Football played on Bn Ground in morning & won by 13/Cheshires. Afternoon of South Lancs beat Bn (Football) 4–2. Evening Bde Boxing Tournament.	
-do-	31		General & Specialist Training – Musketry on 30x Range at CASSEL	

C.W.H. Birt Lt Col
Cdg 8th Bn Border Regt

T2134. Wt. W708–776. 500000. 4/15. Sir J. C. & S.

Instructions regarding War Diaries and Intelligence Summaries are contained in F. S. Regs., Part II. and the Staff Manual respectively. Title pages will be prepared in manuscript.

WAR DIARY
or
INTELLIGENCE SUMMARY.
(*Erase heading not required.*)

Army Form C. 2118.

8 Border Regt

75/75

Vol 24

Place	Date	Hour	Summary of Events and Information 1917	Remarks and references to Appendices
	Sept.			
STEENVORDE	1		Short notice move of Bde to DOMINION CAMP. Bn. left at 12 noon & marched with Bde.	
DOMINION CAMP	2		Church parade. Bn continued march to CH^AU^ SEGARD in DICKEBUSCHE AREA – where went into bivouacs. Enemy aeroplanes heavily bombed surrounding area at night. No casualties.	
CH^AU^ SEGARD	3		C.O's Conference at Bde in morning. Regt Transport moved back to North of DICKEBUSCHE. Bn standing-by.	
-do-	4		Bn. Standing by. Regimental Party reconnoitred Front Line.	
-do-	5		Bn. moved off at 12 noon – relieving 8/L. N. Lanc^s^ in Front Line (Bn. H.Q. at CLAPHAM JUNCTION) with advanced Posts in GLENCORSE WOOD – 150^x^ in front of fairly continuous line. Front about 1400^x^. Relief complete at 10 p.m. Casualties – NIL. Worked all night improving line. Major F. A. WILSON Commt^d^ Bn. Col. C. W. H. BIRT left for week's rest.	
FRONT LINE (in front of) HOODGE	6		Corps (British) on our left attacked some enemy posts – Battle lasted several hours (morning). Light barrage put down by enemy on our left. About noon enemy counter-attacked Corps on our left – light barrage again put down on our left. At 7.15 p.m. enemy appeared to counter attack again – very heavy barrage put down all along our front – but no enemy attack. Barrage lasted 2 hours. All our telephone wires held for 45 minutes – & line to one Coy. for whole time. During night we carried on wiring, making of strong points 100^x^ behind our line (3 such points) – joining up the two Advanced Posts in GLENCORSE WOOD & improving our trenches.	
-do-	7		Quiet day – continued work of night 6/7th	
-do-	8		Quiet day. At 9 p.m. enemy put down heavy barrage on our front – but did not attack. Barrage lasted one hour. Our telephone lines cut after a few minutes. Work continued as above.	
-do-	9		At 4 a.m. enemy put down very heavy barrage on our front – & attacked Bn on our right taking one advanced Post in INVERNESS COPSE. This Bn. (R. W. Kent) counter-attacked at once & retook lost Post – with 12 prisoners. 2/Lt. LANGWORTH killed (Shell-fire). Bn. relieved by 7/London Bn. Relief complete for B Coy (on right) C Coy (Centre) & D Coy (Support) – except for the two Advanced Posts by 6 p.m. Advanced Posts relieved by 10.45 p.m. & remainder of Bn. (A Coy on left & Bn. H.Q.) by 1.30 a.m. on 10/9/17.	
CH^AU^ SEGARD	10		Bn. H.Q. arrived 4 a.m. – found Coys all safely in. At 8.30 a.m. Bn. moved down to WINNIPEG CAMP. During night enemy shelled & bombed CAMP.	
WINNIPEG C^P^	11		Bn. cleaning up & re-organising	
-do-	12		Bn. moved to PRADELLES (by bus)	
PRADELLES	13		Bn. moved (marched) to STEENBECQUE.	
STEENBECQUE	14		Bn. marched to MARLES-LEZ-MINES (about 18 miles). Men marched v. well indeed.	
MARLES-LEZ-MINES	15		Bn. re-organising & cleaning up: also cleaning village & billets wh. were found in a filthy Condition. Lieut-Col. C. W. H. BIRT rejoined Bn.	

23. N. Rebuild

Instructions regarding War Diaries and Intelligence Summaries are contained in F. S. Regs., Part II. and the Staff Manual respectively. Title pages will be prepared in manuscript.

WAR DIARY
or
INTELLIGENCE SUMMARY.
(*Erase heading not required.*)

Army Form C. 2118.

Place	Date	Hour	Summary of Events and Information	Remarks and references to Appendices
MARLES-LEZ-MINES	16/9/17		Church Parade. Brigade Conference	
-do-	17.9.17		General & Specialist Training in morning - Recreational Training in afternoon	
-do-	18.9.17		-do- -do-	
-do-	19.9.17		-do- -do-	
-do-	20/9/17		-do- -do-	
-do-	21/9/17		-do- -do-	
-do-	22.9.17		-do- -do-	
-do-	23.9.17		Church parade -do- -do- Shooting on Range. New Brigade Competition	
-do-	24.9.17		-do- -do-	
-do-	25.9.17		-do- -do-	
-do-	26.9.17		Divisional Sports & fete. Lt Shooting Competition. Wilts 1st Lanc Fus. 2nd Borders 3rd. BORDERS 2nd for Cooker, 3rd for Limber & Water Cart, 3rd for pack mules, 2nd for Tug o' War, 1st Hurdle Race 1st & 2nd Wrestling. 3rd Officers Relay, 2nd Football Kicking. A very successful & pleasant days Sport. 2Lt Drew rejoined Battn from Signal Course.	
NOEUX-LES-MINES	27.9.17		Battalion marched with Brigade (less 8th SL) to NOEUX-LES-MINES. Men in huts, Officers in Billets.	
do.	28.9.17		Resting & cleaning. Advance party under Lt Reed to Cité CALLONE to clean up Dugouts. Battn left NOEUX-LES-MINES at 8pm & marched to CITE CALLONE - Brigade Reserve.	
CITE CALLONE	29.9.17		Cleaning out Cellars. Working parties - deepening & opening up CTs under RE's at night. No Casualties.	
	30.9.17		Improving Dugouts & fitting Gas Blankets. 2 Coys provided Working parties - deepening trenches under REs at night. No Casualties. Major J.S. WILKINSON rejoined Battalion as Second in Command.	

C.W.H. Birt
Lt Col.
Cdg 8th Bn Border Regt

T2134. Wt. W708–776. 500000. 4/15. Sir J. C. & S.

Instructions regarding War Diaries and Intelligence Summaries are contained in F. S. Regs., Part II. and the Staff Manual respectively. Title pages will be prepared in manuscript.

WAR DIARY
or
INTELLIGENCE SUMMARY.
(Erase heading not required.)

Army Form C. 2118.

8th Bn Border Regt.

Vol 25

Place	Date	Hour	Summary of Events and Information	Remarks and references to Appendices
	Oct. 1917			
Cité Calonne	M. 1st		Weather ~~beautiful~~ excellent – usual working parties (2 Coys 100 men each, 7pm, 2 Coys each 100 men 7am). Casualties 2 killed, 5 wounded.	
			C.O., Maj. [illegible] & Capt. [illegible] went round front line 7am – Enemy Aeroplanes fairly active	
	T. 2nd		Weather continued very fine – usual working parties supplied – Aeroplane activity – nil –	
Noeux les Mines	W. 3rd		Fine – Bn moved out into NOEUX LES MINES. Working parties supplied during day.	
	Th. 4th		Day spent cleaning up & resting – Cold & cloudy	
CUINCHY Support	Fri 5th		Bn left at 2pm to march to Le Preol – On arriving at BEUVRY – guides informed C.O. that Bn was to go into trenches – CUINCHY sector – in Bde support	
"			A Coy in front line – B, C & D supports – Day cold – No activity	
"	Sat 6th		Wet & cold –	
"	Sun 7th		Morning fine – Afternoon wet – G.O.C. Bde. also Col. [illegible] – G.O.C. discussed readjustment of Bn arrangements to support the Coy in front line – this to be found by another	
"	~~Mon 8th~~		Bn (2nd S.L.) –	
"	Mon 8th		Fine – Col. Maxwell (2nd S.L.) discussed with C.O. taking over sector occupied by A Coy 8th Border – Arranged to come into effect tomorrow 9th	
"	Tue 9th		Wet in morning – G.O.C. & Brigadier round front line in morning – A Coy relieved by a Coy 2nd S. Lancs – Quiet. 2nd in Comd 2 S. Lancs stopping at Bn HQrs	
"	W. 10th		Wet in morning – fine afternoon – Major MOTT – 2nd in Comd 2 S. Lancs shown round line taken over by his Bn from A Coy – Quiet –	
	T 11th		Wet – Major Denny – 19th Hussars – attached to Bn – 4 Officers – 2/Lts Dowdell – Gibson – Watts – Corley – reported for duty & posted – Quiet –	
LA BASSEE Canal ~~[illegible]~~	F 12th		Wet – Bn was relieved by 2nd S. Lancs – & took over Right sector of Brigade front from 11th Cheshires – Relief complete 2 am. 13th.	
"	Sat 13		Wet – line reconnoitred for organising working parties – Day quiet –	

24. N. 3 sheets

T2134. Wt. W708—776. 500000. 4/15. Sir J. C. & S.

Instructions regarding War Diaries and Intelligence Summaries are contained in F. S. Regs., Part II. and the Staff Manual respectively. Title pages will be prepared in manuscript.

WAR DIARY
or
INTELLIGENCE SUMMARY.
(*Erase heading not required.*)

Army Form C. 2118.

Place	Date	Hour	Summary of Events and Information	Remarks and references to Appendices
LA BASSEE ~~Cuinchy~~ Canal Sector Trenches	Oct 1917			
	Sun 14th		Fine in morning – wet in afternoon – ~~[illegible]~~ received of death of Sgt Cuthbertson C Coy – drowned whilst on course at Corps School at Merville – Quiet. A Coy supplied working parties, 15 to B, 15 to C, 10 to D Coy	
	Mon 15th		Fine. Usual working parties supplied by A Coy – word received of death of Lt Davidson found shot while on course at Army School – Quiet – At night patrol under Lt [illegible] (D Coy) located enemy post & MG post – opposite [illegible] post	
	Tue 16th		Fine: Slight enemy activity – Retaliation by our Stokes – Enemy registered on his own line – our wiring party & reconnoitring patrol prevented by MG gunfire on R sector –	
	Wed 17th		Slight enemy activity – Fine – Enemy aeroplanes active	
	Thurs 18th		Our Artillery bombarded enemy front & support trench – ~~Enemy~~ Enemy retaliated – Bn relieved by 11th Cheshires & moved into reserve at Le Preol	
LE PREOL	Fri 19th		Cleaning up & Baths	
	Sat 20		Baths – Working parties carrying Stokes bombs to trenches – Inter-platoon football	
	Sun 21		REGINA DAY – (21.10.16). Church Parade. Picnic concert by Bn Troupe followed by History of Border Regt by Capt Stewart MC – Working parties supplied	
	Mon 22		Demonstration of wiring by B Coy – Coy training & Inter-platoon football in afternoon – Unsettled weather – Sgts dinner – Lt Col Best went on leave	
	Tue 23		Lecture by Major [illegible] on Trench Discipline – Demonstration of sandbagging by A Coy – Wiring parties practised new GHQ method of apron wire – Coy training & unsettled weather	
Trenches, CANAL Sector – LA BASSEE	Wed 24.		Battn relieved 11th Cheshires in front trenches. relief completed by 10 am. B. A D Compy in front line. C Coy in support.	
			Considerable enemy activity during morning – Morning fine. turned wet in late afternoon –	
	Thur 25th		Fine morning but wet afternoon – Wire cutting shoot by our artillery and Trench mortars from 11.05 to 12.05	
			Gas sent over to enemy's support line from projectors and Stokes mortars at 8.30 pm – Patrols from	
	~~Fri 26th~~		Coy reported little damage done to enemy wire on Battn front	

T2134. Wt. W708–776. 500000. 4/15. Sir J. C. & S.

Instructions regarding War Diaries and Intelligence Summaries are contained in F. S. Regs., Part II. and the Staff Manual respectively. Title pages will be prepared in manuscript.

WAR DIARY
or
INTELLIGENCE SUMMARY.
(Erase heading not required.)

Army Form C. 2118.

Place	Date	Hour	Summary of Events and Information	Remarks and references to Appendices
Trenches. Canal Sector LA BASSEE	Fri. 26th		A wet day - poor visibility - very quiet - usual working parties	
	Sat. 27th		Fine day - Some enemy artillery and aeroplane activity -	
	Sun. 28th		Fine cold day. Our front very quiet - Some trench mortar + artillery activity N of canal.	
	Mon. 29th		Fine day. Artillery activity on both sides above normal - Moon too brilliant for night patrols.	
In support PONT FIXE	Tues. 30th		Some rain. Battn moved into support, being relieved by the 11th Cheshires - relief completed 12.10 pm.	
			B. Coy Marylebone Lane - (support to 11th Cheshires) A Coy Gunner Siding and Hun View. D Coy Keeps	
			C Coy Pont Fixe.	
	Wed. 31st		Very fine day - Considerable artillery activity - Much aerial work on both sides - One British aeroplane	
			brought down on fire behind enemy's line near Canal - Kite baloon brought down near GIVENCHY in flames	
			by enemy planes - Gas alarm sounded about 5.45 pm -	

J S Wilkinson Major

T2134. Wt. W708—776. 500000. 4/15. Sir J. C. & S.

Instructions regarding War Diaries and Intelligence Summaries are contained in F. S. Regs., Part II. and the Staff Manual respectively. Title pages will be prepared in manuscript.

WAR DIARY
or
INTELLIGENCE SUMMARY.
(Erase heading not required.)

Army Form C. 2118.

8th Border Regt.

Vol 26

Place	Date	Hour	Summary of Events and Information	Remarks and references to Appendices
	Novr. 1917.			
In support PONT FIXE	Thur Nov 1st.		Dull day. Normal artillery activity. Conference of Compy Commanders 10. am.	
	Fri. Nov 2nd		Dull day. Great artillery and trench mortar activity throughout day. Normal MG fire during night. No aerial activity.	
	Sat Nov 3rd		Dull day, Normal artillery activity, No Aerial activity. MG's active during evening	
	Sun Nov 4th		Fine, but dull, Very slight artillery activity, No E.A.S seen, slight M.G activity	
LA BASSEE Canal Sector FRONT LINE	Mon Nov 5th		Fine, but dull, Very quiet, Usual working parties found, The batt. relieved the 11th Cheshires in the front line (right sector) 2 Patrols sent out with a view to future operations	
	Tues Nov 6th		Fine, fair observation, 1 of our Planes flying low fired MG into enemy's positions Enemys Aeroplanes inactive also artillery inactive, at 10.30 pm Cloud Gas was discharged from our right, with a gas shell bombardment. Usual patrols sent out.	
	Wed Nov 7th		Fine weather, observation fair, A large number of gas shells were fired into our supports behind the centre company between 2.0 and 3.0 am. Normal Artillery activity during day	25.N.

T2134. Wt. W708—776, 500000. 4/15. Sir J. C. & S.

Instructions regarding War Diaries and Intelligence Summaries are contained in F. S. Regs., Part II. and the Staff Manual respectively. Title pages will be prepared in manuscript.

WAR DIARY
or
INTELLIGENCE SUMMARY.
(Erase heading not required.)

Army Form C. 2118.

Place	Date	Hour	Summary of Events and Information	Remarks and references to Appendices
LA BASSEE CANAL SECTOR FRONT LINE	Thurs Nov 8th		Fine day with good visibility, 3 EA's came over the lines. Hostile Artillery very quiet Our snipers fired 5 shots at a working party. Usual working parties employed	
	Frid Nov 9th		Fine day, cloudy, fair visibility. Our artillery active on enemy front & support line Enemy Artillery inactive until 11.0 pm when he shelled our supports. Normal EA activity. Usual patrols & working parties.	
	Sat Nov 10th		Very wet day until afternoon. At 2.20 am GAS was projected on AUCHY, at the same time 2 fighting patrols went over under cover of smoke, they found no enemy in the front line. Enemy Artillery was very active about noon on the support line behind the right company.	
LE PRÊOL	Sun Nov 11th		Battalion relieved by 11th Cheshires proceeded to LE PRÊOL in reserve. Fine day	
	Mon Nov 12th		Fine day. Cleaning up and Baths 5 days RE Course started for Officers & N C O's	
	Tues Nov 13th		Fine day Coy training. Lectures to platoons by officers. Lecture to N C O's in Canteen	
	Wed Nov 14th		Fine day. Coy training. Lectures to platoons, Lecture to officers, Night Compass March for officers	
	Thurs Nov 15		Fine day. Battalion Parade. Brigadier, Brig Major, M.G. officer & Coy Commanders to dinner	

Instructions regarding War Diaries and Intelligence Summaries are contained in F. S. Regs., Part II. and the Staff Manual respectively. Title pages will be prepared in manuscript.

WAR DIARY
or
INTELLIGENCE SUMMARY.
(Erase heading not required.)

Army Form C. 2118.

Place	Date	Hour	Summary of Events and Information	Remarks and references to Appendices
LE PREOL	Fri Nov 16th		Divine Service, Company Commanders conference at HQ. Football match with RE's at Noeux cancelled owing to casualties in RE team. Battalion Concert, great success.	
LA BASSEE CANAL SECTOR FRONT LINE	Sat Nov 17th		Fine day, fog in morning. Relieved 11th Cheshires in front line by 11.0 am. Mill tunnel and LANE generously treated with Minnies. Both artilleries quiet, Usual patrols and working parties	
	Sun Nov 18th		Fine day, overcast, no rain. Fairly quiet. Our snipers hit 4 Germans, usual working parties. Patrols found 2 Enemy Posts and saw 12 Germans.	
	Mon Nov 19th		Fine day, very cloudy. Artillery fairly active, 2 EA's seen. A patrol of 2nd Lt Hamester, 2nd Lt Robson, a sergeant and a corporal went out. 2nd Lt Robson and the sergeant did not return, it is believed they are captured.	
	Tues Nov 20th		Very dull day, rain commenced about 11.0 pm. Our artillery and TM's carried out a programme from 3.0 pm to 3.45. Enemy Artillery above normal, 5 casualties caused to medium T.M. crews, 1 being killed.	
	Wed Nov 21st		Rainy day, bad observation, Our artillery very quiet. Enemy artillery quiet T.M's very active near Burbure post. Usual working parties. Above normal movement was observed in the enemy lines	

T2134. Wt. W708—776. 500000. 4/15. Sir J. C. & S.

Instructions regarding War Diaries and Intelligence Summaries are contained in F. S. Regs., Part II. and the Staff Manual respectively. Title pages will be prepared in manuscript.

WAR DIARY
or
INTELLIGENCE SUMMARY.
(Erase heading not required.)

Army Form C. 2118.

Place	Date	Hour	Summary of Events and Information	Remarks and references to Appendices
	Thurs 22/11/17		Fine day, but dull, low heavy clouds Our artillery carried out a wire cutting programme astride the BETHUNE - LA BASSEE RD from 12.30 pm to 3.45 pm Enemy artillery very active. 1 EA flew low over our lines firing with his M.G. but doing no damage	
PONT FIXE	Frid 23rd Nov		Fine day. 11th Cheshires relieved us in the front line, while the 8th Borders went into support, very quiet day	
"	Sat 24th Nov		Fine day Our artillery carried out a programme with the T.M's	
"	Sun 25th Nov		Fine day. Fairly quiet, warned to expect a raid on the 7th Brigade front. Did not materialise, expected early in the morning	
"	Mon 26th Nov		Fine day until 11.0 pm when it started snowing which turned into rain Our Artillery carried out an organised shoot. Gas was projected at 8.0 pm on the 74th Bde front. Fairly sharp artillery retaliation by the ~~[illegible]~~ enemy.	
"	Tues Nov 27th		Still raining, colder.	
ANNEZIN	Wed	28.	Bn relieved in Support Line by 6th Lanc. Fusiliers (42nd Div) & moved to ANNEZIN nr BETHUNE - Fine.	
BURBURE.	Thur	29	Brigade Bn moved to BURBURE - (Brigade march) - & marched past G.O.C Division & Brigadier - Fine.	
ERNY ST. JULIEN	Friday	30	Bn marched in Brigade to ERNY ST JULIEN - Inadequate accomodation - Capt Barwell reported from Bde for temporary duty with Bn during training - Showery -	

C W H Birt Lt Col Comdg 8th Border Rgt

T2134. Wt. W708—776. 500000. 4/15. Sir J. C. & S.

SECRET

G.S. 238

Appendix II

8 BN BORDER REGT

Raids – 75th Inf Bde

Night 10/11th November 1917

B.F. 10/11

REPORT UPON RAID on ENEMY TRENCHES by

8th Bn. BORDER Regt. on night Nov. 10th/11th, 1917.

OBJECTS.

1. To secure identification.

2. To inflict casualties.

3. To secure booty.

OBJECTIVES.

Posts in enemy front line at (a) A.21.d.90.65 (VESUVIUS Crater)
(b) A.22.a.05.10.(LA BASSEE Road)

believed to be occupied by enemy were selected as objectives.

RAIDING PARTIES.

2 parties (from A & D Coys.) each divided into 2 sub-parties as follows :-

Sub-party A.	1 Sergt. and 7 O.R.	'A' Coy.
Sub-party B.	1 Officer(2/Lt.C.A.WATTS) & 7 O.R.	'A' Coy.
Sub-party C.	1 Sergt. and 7 O.R.	'D' Coy.
Sub-party D.	1 Officer(2/Lt.T.C. VAUGHAN) & 7 O.R.	'D' Coy.

Objective (a) as above was allotted to sub-parties A & B.

Objective (b) as above was allotted to sub-parties C & D.

The raid was accompanied by a simulated gas attack. Gas projectors and 4" Mortars had the area RYANS KEEP - RAILWAY COTTAGE as a target.

The raid was originally timed to take place at 12.35 a.m. night of 8th/9th Novr. but the wind being unfavourable it was postponed until 1.25 a.m. night of 9th/10th Nov. The wind again being unfavourable it was further postponed until 2.20 a.m. night of 10th/11th November.

Projectors and 4" Mortars were fired at 2.20 a.m. and immediately smoke cases were lit in our front line - the wind being West - 3 - 4 miles per hour. Practically no retaliation resulted, nor any Machine Gun fire. An odd Very Light went up from the enemy line, but on the whole everything was extremely quiet.

SUB-PARTIES A and B.

These parties left our line as per my Battalion Order No.44, copy of which was sent to you - sub-party A making for the South end of Sap at VESUVIUS North and sub-party B. keeping directly to the North of this Sap made straight for the enemy front line. The Sap was found to be occupied by at least two of the enemy, tho' owing to the darkness and the smoke visibility was too uncertain to say exactly by how many more. These two sentries are claimed as casualties by the Sergeant in charge of Party A.

The C.T. connecting (as we supposed) the Sap head with the enemy trench was found to be absolutely filled with wire, and the post completely and effectively surrounded by wire. No other C.T. being discovered by either Party A on the South or by Party B on the North of the Sap xxxx suggests the possibility that the Sap head is connected to the enemy line by tunnel.

Party B (2/Lt. WATTS) found the enemy front line about 5 feet deep but absolutely filled with wire. This was crossed and the party proceeded in a Southerly direction behind the line and could still find no way of getting into the Sap head post on the VESUVIUS CRATER. Talking was heard at the junction of C.T. and front line at A.21.d.9.7. but as the party had already stayed ten minutes after the recall signal, and on account of the wire filled trenches, both A and B parties had to retire without being able to effect any of the desired results. These parties reached our lines soon after 3 a.m., the recall having been given at 2.40 a.m.

SUB-PARTIES C and D.

These parties proceeded as per instructions given in Battalion Order No.44. They found the enemy wire at points of entry into trench no great obstacle (part having been previously cut by hand). Much loose wire was met and the German front line immediately North and South of LA BASSEE ROAD found not only unoccupied but in a state of disrepair and very muddy. No dugout under the Road was located. Covering parties having been left in the front line the rest of the parties proceeded up the short C.T. leading S.E. from A.22.a.12.20. but owing to the mud and the heavy going had only reached the LA BASSEE ROAD when the recall was given. No sign of the enemy was observed though three bombs and several Very Lights came from the direction of FRANKS KEEP - the bombs fell short.

These parties reached our lines at 2.52 a.m., the recall having been given at 2.40 a.m.

The 'Officers Call' on the bugle was the Signal of Recall.

The wind was scarcely strong enough to carry the smoke cloud across to the enemy lines as had been hoped, it being about our trenches so much that fewer cases were lit. Though he heard a bell being rung 2nd Lieut.WATTS does not think the smoke cloud deceived the enemy - the reflection of the smoke case burning in our trenches could be seen from the enemy front line.

We suffered no casualties.

(sd). C.W.H. Birt, Lieut. Col.,
11/11/17. Commanding 8th Bn. Border Regt.

S E C R E T

25th Division G.S.238.

XI Corps.

Herewith copy of Report by O.C. 8th Bn BORDER Regiment on the raid carried out by his Battalion on night 10th/11th November, for your information.

Sd O. H. Nicholson Lt Col
for G.O.C.

12/11/17. Commanding 25th Division.

HEADQUARTERS,
GENERAL STAFF,
25TH DIVISION.
No. GS238
Date 11.11.17.

GOC
To see
on

SECRET.

25th Division 'G'.

BM. R. 848.

Herewith report by O.C., 8th Border Regt., on raid carried out night 10th/11th November.

WRD Cattie
Capt for
Brigadier-General,

11/11/1917. Commanding 75th Infantry Brigade.

G.O.C. seen 11/11/17
G.S.O. I.
G.S.O. II.
G.S.O. III.
A.A.&Q.M.G.

S E C R E T.

25th Division No: G.S. 238.

XI Corps.
46th Division.
1st Portuguese Division.

Reference 25th Division No: G.S. 238 of 8th November - provided the wind is favourable the operation will be carried out tonight, 10th/11th November.

Zero hour will be 2.20 a.m.

All other arrangements will be as stated in 25th Division letters No: G.S. 238 dated 8th and 9th November.

(Sd) O.H.L. Nicholson, Lieut-Colonel
for Major General,
Commanding 25th Division.

10th Novr. 1917.

Copy to Corps H.Q.

S E C R E T.

B.O./206/4.

Reference Brigade Order No. 206 dated 6th November, 1917.

Provided the wind is favourable the operation will take place to-night, 10th/11th November.

ZERO hour will be 2.20 a.m.

All other arrangements will be the same as for last night, 9th/10th November.

ACKNOWLEDGE.

K.F.D. Gattie

Captain,

10th November, 1917. Brigade Major, 75th Infantry Brigade.

Copies to :-

25th Division 'G'.
7th Infantry Brigade.
74th Infantry Brigade.
C.R.A., 25th Division.
11th Cheshire Regt.
8th Border Regt.
2nd S. Lancs Regt.
8th S. Lancs Regt.
75th T.M. Battery.
75th M.G. Company.
110th Brigade R.F.A.
No: 4 Special Coy. R.E.
'D' Special Coy. R.E.
75th Field Ambulance.
75th Bde: Signals.
106th Field Coy. R.E.
G.O.C.
Staff Captain.
War Diary.
File.

83/

SECRET.

25th Division No: G.S.238/A.

XI Corps.
46th Division.
1st Portuguese Division.

....

Reference 25th Division No: G.S.238 of to-day.

Zero hour will be...1.25 a.m......

Please acknowledge.

[signature] Capt.
for Major General,
Commanding 25th Division.

9th November, 1917.

S E C R E T.

B.C.206/3.

Reference Brigade Order No. 206 dated 6th November, 1917.

Provided the wind is favourable the operation will take place to night, 9th/10th November.

ZERO hour will be ....1·25 a.m.

Corps, Flank Divs notified.

All other arrangements will be the same as for last night, 8th/9th November.

Acknowledged.

K.F.D. Gattie

Captain,

9th November, 1917. Brigade Major, 75th Infantry Brigade.

Copies to:-

25th Division "G". ✓ C.R.A. 25th Division.
7th Infantry Brigade.
74th Infantry Brigade.
11th Cheshire Regt.
8th Border Regt.
2nd S.Lancs. Regt.
8th S.Lancs. Regt.
75th T.M.Battery.
75th M.G.Company.
110th Brigade R.F.A.
No. 4 Special Coy. R.E.
'D' Special Coy. R.E.
75th Field Ambulance.
75th Bde. Signals.
106th Field Coy. R.E.
G.O.C.
Staff Captain.
War Diary.
File.

S E C R E T

25th Division G.S.238.

XI Corps.
46th Division.
1st Portuguese Division.

1. Reference 25th Division G.S.238 of the 8th November - owing to unfavourable wind the raid did not take place on the night 8th/9th November.

2. The raid will be carried out tonight 9th/10th November, or should the wind be unfavourable for the operation, on the first succeeding favourable night. New zero hour will be notified later.

3. Codes to be used are:-

ALL SWANK - Operation will take place tonight.

EXEMPT - Operation will not take place tonight.

A.L. Nicholson Lt-Colgs
Major General,
Commanding 25th Division.

9th Novr 1917.

Copy to:-
C.R.A., 25th Division.

Map ref:
LA BASSEE; 1/10,000

SECRET

Copy No. 2
Nov. 8th 1917

No.4SPECIAL COMPANY, R.E. OPERATION ORDER No. 104.

1. Intention: In order to assist a raid by 8th Border Regt. on enemy trenches:-
(a) Post at A.21.d.65.65., (b) Front line from A.22.c.0.9. to A.22.a.05.15
"O"Section, No.4 Special Coy. R.E. will co-operate in a similated gas attack by firing gas bombs on to RYANS KEEP at zero hour, in conjunction with Projectors of "D"Special Coy. R.E. and Smoke candles to be liberated by Infantry.

2. Detail: No. of Mortars; 6
Emplacements; at about A.21.d.7.6.
Target; RYANS KEEP.
Ammunition; T.M.E., C.G. - 100 rounds.
T.M.E., N.C. - 100 rounds.

3. Zero hour will be 12.35 a.m., Nov.8/9th.

4. Wind limits; W.N.W. thro' W. to S.W.

5. CODE: The following Code will be used;
Operation will take place to-night; ALL SWANK
" will not " " " ; EXEMPT

6. Light Signals:
(a) Succession of GREEN Verey lights fired from A.21.d.30.85. in the LANE by O.C. Raid at zero - 10 mins:- Operation WILL NOT take place to-night.
(b) Succession of GREEN Verey lights fired by O.C. Raid on completion of raid:- Raid complete, ALL CLEAR.

7. Decisions: O.C. "O" Section will be at Battn. H.Q. at BRADDELL POINT at zero - 2 hours, when a decision will be made by O.C. Battn.: if this is favourable O.C. "O" Section will report to O.C. Raid at A.21.d.30.85. in the LANE by zero - 30 mins. at latest. At zero - 10 mins. O.C. Raid will make a decision in consultation with O.C. "O" Section and O.C. "D" Special Coy. R.E. O.C. "O" Section will take the firing of "D" Special Coy's Projectors as a signal for opening fire: all rounds to be fired in one burst of rapid fire.

8. Precautions: It is advised that personnel ~~should~~ wear box respirators and gas doors be closed from zero-5mins. till ALL CLEAR is given within the line of fire of the Mortars. O.C. "O" Section will detail an Officer to inspect the front line immediately after ceasing fire, who will report when all is clear: O.C. "O" Section will then inform the Coy. H.Q. in ROBERTSON'S Tunnel and wire PRIORITY to Battn. H.Q.

P.T.O.

O.O.104 (contd) Sheet 2

9. Synchronisation: O.C. "O" Section will synchronise his time with that of Battn. H.Q., BRADDELL POINT before the operation.

10. ACKNOWLEDGE.

A. Rathbone
Capt
O.C. No.4 Special Coy. R.E.

Issued at 5.15pm.

Copies to:- No. 1 XI Corps.
2 25th Division.
3 75th Inf. Bde.
4/5 O.C. "O" Section, No.4 Spec.Coy.
6 O.C. "D" Special Coy. R.E.
7 O.C. No.4 " " "
8 C.S.C., R.E., First Army.
9 File.
10/11 War Diary.

"D" Special Coy RE

Operation Order No 31

Reference Map:- La Bassee 36c N.W.1 Copy No 4

1. A raid will take place on night 8/9 Nov: 1917 on 75th Inf Bde front if wind and weather conditions are favourable. In conjunction with this there will be a simulated cylinder discharge by means of smoke candles from the front line and "D" Special Coy will project 200 drums "CG"
2. Sections 16 and 19 under 2/Lts Daniels and Bishop will install 100 projectors each.
3. Projector position is about A27 a 9.9.
4. Target is A28 b central
5. Wind limits are:- WSW through W to W.N.W.
6. The firing of projectors will be the signal for smoke candles to be lit.
7. Os C Sections 16 and 19 will wire wind readings in code to Lt Saunders (who will be at Bn HQrs BRADDELL POINT) addressed "George C/O CB35 These will be sent at the following times - Zero minus 2½ hrs, minus 2 hrs, minus 1hr, minus ½ hr
8. The following code will be used:-

   Operation will take place tonight = AHH SWANK

   Operation will not take place tonight = EXEMPT.

   Projectors discharged - all clear = FIT.

In the event of the wind becoming unfavourable by Zero minus 10 minutes light Signals will be used. Os C Sns 16+19 will make arrangements for careful look-out to be kept for these signals and will act accordingly:-

Succession of GREEN Verey lights fired from the junction of the front line and the LA BASSEE Road by O.C. Raiders at Zero minus 10 minutes = Operation will not take place tonight

(Continued)

9. The following precautions will be taken by the troops in the line.
All within the following area will wear box respirators from Zero minus 5 mins till ordered by their officer to remove them – after receipt of "all clear" viz:–
Junction of TOWER RESERVE and ROBERTSON'S ALLEY East to front line.
KINGSWAY – ARTHUR'S KEEP – A 27 b 0.2 to A27 d 9.8.

10. OsC. Sections 16 and 19 will each detail an orderly to report at BRADDELL POINT with watches at 7.30 pm. 8/11/17.

11. Zero hour will be 12.35 am 9/11/17.

(Sd) A G Saunders Lt RE
Comdg D Special Coy RE

Issued at 2.0 pm 8/11/17 to:–

1 CSCRE 1st army
2 75th Inf Bde
3 74th " "
4 25th Division
5 O.C. Section 16
6 " " 19
7 } War Diary
8 }
9 File

ackd [illegible]

Goc To see on.

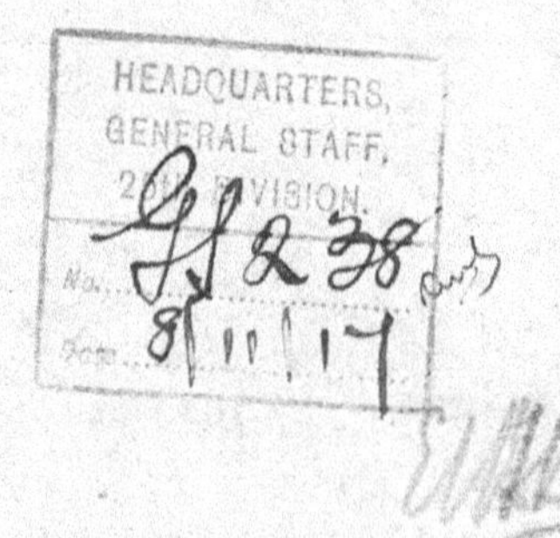

S E C R E T. B.M.1/27.

O.C.112th Brigade. R. F. A.

1. The 75th Infantry Brigade is carrying out a raid tonight on the enemy's trench at A.21.d.8565 and from A.22.c.0.9. - A.22.a.0515.

2. The raid will be accompanied by a simulated gas attack and will therefore be dependent on the wind.

3. There will be no artillery bombardment, but 110th Brigade R.F.A. will be in readiness to put down a barrage to cover the withdrawal of the raiders if necessary.

The signal for this barrage will be a GOLD and SILVER Rain Rocket fired from the LANE A.21.d.3085 and repeated at BRADDELL POINT.

4. The 112th Brigade. R.F.A. will assist with 4.5" Hows firing gas (B C B R) on the following M.G. emplacements :-

A.16.c.7.4.
A.16.d.6500.
A.22.b.2575.
A.22.b.5540.
A.22.b.8463.
A.22.b.0.1.

This will commence at ZERO.

TIME TABLE.

From.	To.	Rate per how p.m.	Rounds per How. BCBR	HE.
Zero.	Plus 4.	3.	12	
Plus 4.	Plus 20.	1.		16.
Plus 20.	Plus 24.	3.	12.	

5. At Zero minus 30 minutes the 112th Brigade R.F.A. will fire 3 rounds per gun on their harassing fire targets.

6. On the signal mentioned in para 3 being fired, the 112th Brigade will fire with bursts of Harassing fire for 10 minutes.

7. ZERO HOUR will be 12-35.a.m. tonight 8th/9th November.

8. In case it in necessary to cancel the operation the word EXEMPT will be wired from D.A.H.Q.

9. White Very Lights will be fired from BRADDELL POINT during the operation as a guide for direction for the raiders.

These lights must not be confused with the GOLD and SILVER Rain ROCKET.

10. ACKNOWLEDGE.

Major. R.A.
Brigade Major. 25th Div. Artillery

Copies to 25th Div. G.
75th Inf Bde.
110th ...

SECRET

B.O.206/2.

AMENDMENTS to 75th INFANTRY BRIGADE ORDER No.206/1 dated 7th Novr.

Para: 3,(a) and the last 3 lines of para. 5 of 75th Infantry Brigade Order No, 206/1 dated 7th November are cancelled and the following substituted :-

Representatives of No. 4 and "D" Special Companies R.E. will meet the O.C. Raiders in the LANE, Communication Trench at A.21.d.30.85. at Zero minus 30 minutes and from this point will fire up a succession of GREEN Very Lights at Zero minus 10 minutes in the event of the wind having become in their opinion unfavourable.

Reference para: 5, (b) and (c) of Brigade Order No. 206/1, these light signals will still hold good as at present arranged except that they will be fired up from the LANE at A.21.d.30.85 instead of from the junction of the front line and the LA BASSEE ROAD.

ACKNOWLEDGED.
WHB

KFD Gattie
Captain,

8th November,1917. Brigade Major, 75th Infantry Brigade.

Copies to :-
25th Division "G".
7th Infantry Brigade.
74th Infantry Brigade.
11th Cheshire Regt.
8th Border Regt.
2nd S.Lancs. Regt.
8th S. Lancs. Regt.
5th Bn. C.E.P.
75th T.M.Battery.
75th M.G.Company.
110th Brigade R.F.A.
No. 4 Special Coy. R.E.
'D' Special Coy. R.E.
75th Field Ambulance.
75th Bde. Signals.
G.O.C.
War Diary.
File.
106th Field Coy. R.E.

S E C R E T.

25th Division No: G.S. 238.

XI Corps.
46th Division.
1st Portuguese Division.

Reference Map 1/10,000 LA BASSEE (Sh. 36^{c} N.W.1).

****

1. A raid will be carried out tonight by the 8th Bn: Border Regiment (75th Infantry Brigade) on the following objective :-

(a) The portion of the enemy trench at about A.21.d.85.65 where an enemy post is suspected.

(b) The enemy front line astride the LA BASSEE road from A.22.c.00.90 to A.22.a.05.15 where certain posts have been located and a machine gun is suspected.

2. The raid will be accompanied by a simulated gas projector attack, the firing of gas bombs from 4" Mortars and shelling of the enemy's defences with gas shells. The operation is, therefore, dependent on the wind.

The raiders will enter the enemy's defences under cover of a smoke cloud.

3. There will be no artillery bombardment but the Artillery and Stokes Mortars will be prepared to put down a barrage, ifnecessary, to cover the withdrawal of the raiding party. The signal for this barrage will be a Gold and Silver rain Rocket.

4. Zero hour will be 12.35 a.m. night 8th/9th November.

Capt.
for Major General,

8th November, 1917. Commanding 25th Division.

G.O.C.
G.S.O. I.
G.S.O. II.
G.S.O. III.
A.A. & Q.M.G.

S E C R E T.

COPY NO. 1

75th INFANTRY BRIGADE ORDER NO. 206/1.

7th November, 1917.

1. Reference 75th Infantry Brigade Order No. 206 dated 6/11/17. ZERO hour is fixed for 12.35 a.m. night 8th/9th November.

2. Following code messages will be used in connection with the operation :-

ALL SWANK :- Operation will take place to-night.

EXEMPT. - Operation will NOT take place tonight.

3. Following light signals will be used in connection with the operation :-

(a). Succession of GREEN Verey Lights fired from the junction of the Front Line and the LA BASSEE ROAD by O.C. Raiders at ZERO minus 10 minutes = OPERATION WILL NOT TAKE PLACE TO-NIGHT.

(b). Succession of GREEN Verey Lights fired by O.C. Raiders from same position, on completion of raid = RAID COMPLETE - ALL CLEAR.

(c). The Gold and Silver Rain rocket referred to in para: 4 of Brigade Order No. 206. This will be fired from the same position as mentioned above and will also be repeated at BRADDELL POINT.

(d). Ordinary WHITE Verey Lights will be fired up from BRADDELL POINT during the raid as an indication of direction to the Raiders.

4. O.C., 75th T.M. Battery, O.C., No. 4 Special Co., R.E., and O.C., 'D' Special Co., R.E., will be at Headquarters, 8th Border Regt., at BRADDELL POINT.

5. At ZERO minus 2 hours, O.C. 8th Borders will make a decision in consultation with O.C., No. 4 Special Co. R.E., and O.C. 'D' Special Co., R.E., as to whether the wind is favourable or not for the operation, and will notify his decision to Brigade Head Quarters by means of code messages referred to in para: 2.
If by ZERO minus 10 minutes the wind has become unfavourable, O.C. Raiders will be empowered to fire up the GREEN Lights referred to in para. 3.

6. Brigade Signal Officer will make any additional signal arrangements that may be necessary for the purpose of enabling O.C., 75th T.M. Battery and O's. C. No. 4 and 'D' Special Co's., R.E. to keep in touch with their respective Section Officers.

7. Brigade Signal Officer will send a watch shewing correct time to Headquarters, 8th Border Regt., and to Headquarters, 110th Brigade, R.F.A., by 8 p.m. November 8th.

8. ACKNOWLEDGED

K.F.D. Gattie
Captain,
Brigade Major, 75th Infantry Brigade.

Issued through Signals at 8.40 p.m.

Copies to :-

25th Division 'G'. ✓
7th Infantry Brigade.
74th Infantry Brigade.
11th Cheshire Regt.
8th Border Regt.
2nd S. Lancs Regt.
8th S. Lancs Regt.
5th Bn: C.E.P.
75th T.M. Battery.
75th M.G. Company.
110th Brigade, R.F.A.
No. 4 Special Co., R.E.
'D' Special Co., R.E.
75th Field Ambulance.
75th Bde: Signals.
G.O.C.
Staff Captain.
War Diary.
File.
106th Field Coy. R.E.

"A" Form
Army Form C. 2121
(In pads of 100)

MESSAGES AND SIGNALS.

No. of Message..............

Prefix............ Code..................m. | Words. Charge. | This message is on a/c of: | Recd. at...........m.

Office of Origin and Service Instructions | Sent | ....Service. | Date......................

At....................m. | From....................

To........................

By........................ | (Signature of "Franking Officer.") | By........................

TO Q

Sender's Number.	Day of Month.	In reply to Number.	AAA
* GS 238	7/11		

Reference	para	1	of
GS 238	of	6/11/17	Corps
have	authorized	issue	of
700	single	smoke	cases
type	"S"	&	100
[illegible]	Bombs	under	SS 1244/69/2
of	7/11/17	aaa	will
you	please	issue.	to
75th	Bde	as	soon
as	possible		

From G
Place
Time 5 45 pm

The above may be forwarded as now corrected.
(Z) [illegible signature]
.... Censor.
Signature of Addressor or person authorised to telegraph in his name.

* This line should be erased if not required.

(7981) Wt. W493/M1647 130,000 Pads 5/17 D. D. & L. E1187

HEADQUARTERS,
GENERAL STAFF,
25th DIVISION.
No. G.S 238
Date 7/11/17

GS1 BSec 868

S E C R E T.

XI Corps.
SS.1214/69/2.

25th Division.

With reference to your G.S.238 dated 6th November, 1917.

Sanction has now been granted for issue of stores mentioned in para. 1 of your letter.

These stores are being issued to you as soon as possible.

The issue of the ammunition asked for in para. 2 has already been approved.

M. Henderson Major
G.S

XI CORPS.
7.11.17.

for B. G., G. S.

"C" Form.

MESSAGES AND SIGNALS.

Army Form C. 2123.
(In books of 100.)

No. of Message

Prefix ~ Code ~ Words 16

£ s. d.

Charges to Collect

Service Instructions

Received. From ADO By JB

Sent, or sent out. At m. To By

Office Stamp. [stamp: YBE -- 7.XI.17. TELEGRAPHS]

Handed in at Lis Office 10.1 a.m. Received 10.25 a.m.

TO 25 Divn

Sender's Number.	Day of Month.	In reply to Number.	AAA
G 472	7	G 536	

Para	2	aaa	issue
of	200	drums CG	
approved			

Copy sent to O.C. D.

Special Coy R.E. 7/11/17

10.35 a.m.

FROM II Corps

TIME & PLACE

*This line should be erased if not required.

100,000.—John Rissen, Ltd.—3/17.—3141. Forms C2123.

SECRET.

COPY NO. 1.

75TH INFANTRY BRIGADE ORDER NO. 206.

Reference Map :-
1/10,000 LA BASSEE (Sheet 36c N.W.1.) 6th November, 1917.

1. A raid will be carried out by the 8th Borders on a date and at a time to be notified later.
The raid will be accompanied by a simulated gas attack and will therefore be dependent on the wind; all arrangements will however be made for carrying out the operation on the evening of Thursday, November 8th, if conditions are favourable.

2. The objectives are as follows :-

(a). The portion of the enemy trench at about A.21.d.85.65. where an enemy post is suspected.

(b). The enemy front line astride the LA BASSEE Road from A.22.c.0.9. to A.22.a.05.15. where certain posts have been located and a machine gun is suspected.

3. At Zero, projectors will project gas into the area RYANS KEEP - FRANKS KEEP - RAILWAY COTTAGE.
The firing of the projectors will be the signal for smoke candles to be lit along the whole front from TWIN SAP to ARGYLE SAP SOUTH under arrangements of O.C. 8th Borders, and also for 4" Mortars to fire gas bombs into the area RYANS KEEP - FRANKS KEEP - RAILWAY COTTAGE.
Under cover of this smoke cloud, the raiding parties will effect an entry into the enemy trenches.

4. There will be no Artillery bombardment, but from Zero onwards, the Artillery will stand by in readiness to put down, if necessary, a barrage to cover the withdrawal of the raiders, and four 3" Stokes Mortars will similarly be prepared to co-operate on selected points in enemy trenches (to be mutually decided between O.C. 75th T.M. Battery and O.C. 8th Borders.).
The signal for the Artillery and 3" Mortars to open fire will be, a gold and silver rain rocket, fired up by the O.C. Raiders from a point to be selected by O.C. 8th Borders, and to be notified to all concerned.

5. Officers Commanding 110th Brigade, R.F.A., 8th Borders, No. 4 Special Coy. R.E., 'D' Special Coy. R.E., and 75th T.M. Battery, will submit their plans in accordance with the above by noon to-morrow.

6. ACKNOWLEDGE.d

K F D Gattie
Captain,
Brigade Major, 75th Infantry Brigade.

Issued at 7.30 p.m.
Copies to :-

25th Division 'G'.	75th M.G. Company.
7th Infantry Brigade.	110th Brigade, R.F.A.
74th Infantry Brigade.	No. 4 Special Coy. R.E.
11th Cheshire Regt.	'D' Special Coy. R.E.
8th Border Regt.	75th Field Ambulance.
2nd S. Lancs Regt.	G.O.C.
8th S. Lancs Regt.	Staff Captain.
5th Bn: C.E.P.	War Diary.
75th T.M. Battery.	File.

Army Form C. 2123.
(In books of 100.)

"C" Form.

MESSAGES AND SIGNALS.

No. of Message

Prefix Code Words | Received. | Sent, or sent out. | Office Stamp.

£ s. d.

Charges to Collect | From | At m. | ARMY YBE --6.XI.17. TELEGRAPHS

By | To

Service Instructions. 1 of 2 adds

By

Handed in at AAK Office 6.55 p m. Received 11.10 p m.

TO 25 Divn

*Sender's Number.	Day of Month.	In reply to Number.	AAA
G943	6/11		

At	request	of	CYCLAMEN
issue	of	following	is
approved	aaa	TMECG	100
aaa	TMENC	100	aaa
application	should	have	come
through	you	addsd	11
Corps	reptd	HQ	special
Coys	RE	and	25
Division			

HEADQUARTERS, GENERAL STAFF. 25th DIVISION.
No. G946
Date 6/11/17

FROM First Army

TIME & PLACE 10/45 pm

*This line should be erased if not required.

100,000.—John Rissen, Ltd.—2/17.—8141 Forms C2123.

GOC
To see

SECRET.

25th Division No: G.S. 238.

XI Corps.

1. May 700 single smoke cases type 'S' and 100 'P' bombs be issued to this Division for a minor operation?

2. Authority is also requested for the issue of 200 drums of 'C.G.' ammunition to "D" Special Company R.E.

These are required in connection with a raid by the 75th Infantry Brigade, which it is hoped to carry out two days after the present gas operations have taken place. By projecting gas again against the vicinity of AUCHY after an interval of only two days, it is thought that good results may be obtained, as the enemy may not be expecting gas again so soon and, in addition, it will assist the raid considerably by causing confusion in the rear just when the raid is taking place.

[signature] Capt
for Major General,

6th November, 1917. Commanding 25th Division.

113

(6202) W 11186/M1151 350,000 12/16 McA. & W., Ltd. (Est. 781) Forms/W 3091/3. Army Form W. 3091.

Cover for Documents.

Nature of Enclosures.

Movements

Concentration

Method of moving by train and Bus.

Rules for Marching:

Arty & S.A.A sections of Divl Amm Columns

Notes, or Letters written.

Instructions regarding War Diaries and Intelligence Summaries are contained in F. S. Regs., Part II. and the Staff Manual respectively. Title pages will be prepared in manuscript.

WAR DIARY
or
INTELLIGENCE SUMMARY.
(Erase heading not required.)

Army Form C. 2118.

8th Bn Border Regt.

Vol 27

Place	Date	Hour	Summary of Events and Information	Remarks and references to Appendices
	Dec 1917			
ERNY ST JULIEN	Sat 1st		Cleaning up billets & Coy inspections - Cold & showery.	
	Sun 2nd		No church parade - owing to Chaplain having left Bn through sickness -	
	Mon 3rd		Bn preparing to move to 3rd Army Area - D Coy proceeded as Loading Coy at ANVIN -	
	Tue 4th		A Coy left 1.45 am - Remainder Transport 5.0 am - Remainder 7.45 am. Left ERNY ST JULIEN & marched to ANVIN - Entraining for ACHIET LE GRAND (3rd Army Area) - Arrived 11.30 pm & marched to GOMIECOURT - Freezing.	
GOMIECOURT / ROCQUIGNY	Wed 5th		Cold night in huts at GOMIECOURT - Marched in Bde to Huts at ROCQUIGNY - via BAPAUME - Cold but fine.	
	Thu 6th		Cleaning up - & Coy inspections - Showery	
	Fri 7th		Coy training - & Lewis Gun classes - Wet	
	Sat 8th		Cold & showery. - Lt Col Sir W Lennard Bt (ADC 6th Corps) - late 2nd i/c Cmd visited Bn - Concert at night & Coy training - musketry & Bombing.	
ROCQUIGNY / BEUGNATRE	Sun 9th		Bn marched as Brigade to BEUGNATRE - in huts - Bde in Divl reserve - Wet -	
	Mon 10th		Coy training - Lewis Gun class	
	Tues 11th		Bn found working parties for burying cable. Weather cold, hard frost at night	
	Wed 12th		- do - - do -	
	Thurs 13th		- do - - do -	
	Fri 14th		- do - - do -	
	Sat 15th		- do - - do -	
	Sun 16th		Bn attended Divine Service. Weather cold & frosty but fine.	26.N. 2 sheets

T2134. Wt. W708—776 500000. 4/15. Sir J. C. & S.

Instructions regarding War Diaries and Intelligence Summaries are contained in F. S. Regs., Part II. and the Staff Manual respectively. Title pages will be prepared in manuscript.

WAR DIARY
or
INTELLIGENCE SUMMARY.
(Erase heading not required.)

Army Form C. 2118.

Place	Date	Hour	Summary of Events and Information	Remarks and references to Appendices
BEUGNATRE.	Mon 17th		Bn engaged on working parties burying cable. Slight fall of snow. weather cold.	
	Tues 18th		Bn engaged on working parties burying cable. Weather extremely cold. Freezing hard.	
	Wed 19th		Bn engaged on working parties burying cable. Weather cold & frosty	
	Th. 20		Cleaning up billets. Company Inspections. Company Commanders reconnoitre trenches.	
LAGNICOURT	Fr. 21st		Bn relieved 4th Bn South Staffs Regt in the line N.E of LAGNICOURT. No casualties.	
	Sat 22nd		Very quiet. Good work done during day improving & deepening trenches in places. Wiring at night.	
	Sun 23		Quiet day. LAGNICOURT shelled fairly heavily by hostile artillery. Wire in front strengthened. Freezing.	
	Mon 24		50 men (A Coy) digging new Support Line from HARROGATE AVENUE [illegible] to YORK SUPPORT 5pm - 9pm - freezing	
	Tue 25th		Xmas day - Enemy shelled Harrogate Av. Nr Bn HQrs - wounded 2 Cheshire men - Snow during day - 2 [illegible] on night - on working duty - lost during snowfall - not returned - Brigadier visited Bn - to [illegible] compliments of the season -	
	Wed 26th		Quiet day - fine	
VAULX-VRAUCOURT	Thur 27		Bn moved to VAULX - VRAUCOURT -	
	Fr. 28th		Cleaning up - Coy inspections - & baths - fine - freezing	
	Sat 29th		2 Coys wiring MORCHIES-VAUX line - 2 Coys digging deepening & improving LAGNICOURT SWITCH - fine & cold.	
	Sun 30th		Usual working parties -	
	Mon 31st		Fine - usual working parties - fine & cold.	

C W A Bird Lt Col
Comdg 8th Borders.

Instructions regarding War Diaries and Intelligence Summaries are contained in F. S. Regs., Part II. and the Staff Manual respectively. Title pages will be prepared in manuscript.

WAR DIARY
or
INTELLIGENCE SUMMARY.
(Erase heading not required.)

Army Form C. 2118.

8 Bn Border Regt

Vol 28

~~January~~ 1918

Place	Date	Hour	Summary of Events and Information	Remarks and references to Appendices
VRAUCOURT	Tue 1st		Bn still in reserve occupying [illegible] Day fine. Quiet	
BEUGNATRE	Wed 2nd		Bn relieved by 4th South Staffs - relief completed by midday	
"	Thu 3rd		Cleaning up & Coy inspections - Col Bart went on 3 days Course to R.F.C.	
"	Fri 4th		Cleaning up billets - Xmas day festivities held to day - Day Quiet	
"	Sat 5th		Heavy [illegible] between 5 30 & 6 30 a.m.	
"	Sun 6		Church Parade - Special Intercession service - Quiet - fine	
"	Mon 7		Practice attack by A Coy on pill boxes - Other Coys - Range & Coy training	
"	Tue 8		Practice attack by A & C Coys on pill boxes - Brigadier & C/ B Major present - Operation done in blizzard - Other Coys Coy training & Baths	
"	Wed 9		B Coy practice attack on Pill Boxes - Wild weather - Aeroplane fire. Squadron compelled to land [illegible] 2 Officers stayed to tea [illegible]	
"	Thur 10		Working party on [illegible] men - New Chaplain for 2 Sh & 8 Borders - Rev Capt Scott came to lunch	
"	Fri 11		Usual Coy parades - Wild & unsettled weather	
"	Sat 12		[illegible] Staff Officer & Staff Capt. [illegible] Camp - & promised 20 extra huts for Men, 2 for Officers & 3 Cookhouses	
"	Sun 13		Church Parade [illegible] - Cold & wet in morning	
LAGNICOURT	Mon 14		Bn relieved 1st South Staffs in line. Relief complete 7 30 - Cold & dry - [illegible] A Coy left, B Coy R, C left Support, D Right Support	
"	Tue 15		Work continued on new Cookhouses for 2 front line Coys (under R.E.'s) - Also sinking of well - Day - fine turning to rain later	
"	Wed 16		Trenches in shocking condition - much falling in during night - Day wet & misty - frost in evening turning to rain about midnight	
"	Thur 17		Work on cookhouses temporarily abandoned - occasional rain	
"	Fri 18		Unsettled weather in morning - [illegible]	
"	Sat 19		Unsettled weather. Enemy artillery active on "A" Coys sector and around Bn Hdqrs on Sunken road. 3 men wounded by shell at Bn Hdqrs.	
"	Sun 20		Fine morning. Unsettled in afternoon. Quiet. Vicinity of Bn Hdqrs occasionally shelled. Bn relieved by 2nd Bn South Lancs and moved into support.	
"	Mon 21		One Coy (D) in support to right Bn, one coy (C) in support to left Bn. Both coys at tactical disposal of O.C. front line Bns. No casualties during relief. Remaining two coys employed in clearing trenches of left Bn and carrying timber from R.E. dump for Tunnelling Coy.	
"	Tues 22nd		Employed clearing trenches &c	
	Wed 23rd		— do —	

27. N.
2 sheets

A7092). Wt. W12839/M1293 750,000. 1/17. D. D & L., Ltd. Forms/C2118/14.

Instructions regarding War Diaries and Intelligence Summaries are contained in F. S. Regs., Part II. and the Staff Manual respectively. Title pages will be prepared in manuscript.

WAR DIARY
or
INTELLIGENCE SUMMARY.

(Erase heading not required.)

Army Form C. 2118.

Place	Date January 1918	Hour	Summary of Events and Information	Remarks and references to Appendices
Lagnicourt	Thurs 24th		One company working with Tunnelling Coy. One Coy carrying for R.Es. remaining two companies employed clearing & cleaning up communication & support line trenches.	
	Fri 25th		— do —	
	Sat 26th		Relieved in support by 4th Bn South Staff Regt and moved back into reserve. Quiet relief. Enemy sent some tear shells into vicinity of LAGNICOURT.	
	Sun 27th		Bn found working parties amounting to 332 men, digging & wiring. Church service in camp on afternoon.	
	Mon 28th		332 men on digging, remainder working on improvements to camp	
	Tues 29th		— do — — do — — do —	
	Wed 30th		— do — — do — — do —	
	Thurs 31st		— do — — do — — do —	

C W H Burt
Lt Col.
Cdg 8th Bn Border Regt
1/2/18

A7092). Wt. W12839/M1293 750,000. 1/17. D. D & L., Ltd. Forms/C2118/14.

Instructions regarding War Diaries and Intelligence Summaries are contained in F. S. Regs., Part II. and the Staff Manual respectively. Title pages will be prepared in manuscript.

February

WAR DIARY
or
INTELLIGENCE SUMMARY.
(Erase heading not required.)

Army Form C. 2118.

8 Bn Border Regt

Vol 29

Place	Date	Hour	Summary of Events and Information	Remarks and references to Appendices
BEUGNATRE	Fri 1st		5 Officers & 250 Other Ranks employed on VAULX-MORCHIES line digging. Remainder of Battalion employed on improvement of camp.	
"	Sat 2nd		5 Officers and 250 Other Ranks employed on VAULX-MORCHIES line wiring under R.E. supervision. Remainder of Battalion employed on improvement of camp.	
"	Sun 3rd		5 Officers and 250 other Ranks employed on VAULX-MORCHIES line digging under RE supervision. Remainder of Battalion employed on improvement of camp. C of E service in camp at 5-30 p.m.	
"	Mon 4th		5 Officers and 200 other Ranks employed on VAULX-MORCHIES line wiring under supervision of RE. Remainder of battalion paraded at 9-30 am for Ceremonial Drill, remainder of morning under Company Commanders.	
"	Tue 5th		5 Officers and 200 other Ranks employed on VAULX-MORCHIES line digging under R.E. supervision. Remainder of battalion employed on improvement of camp.	
"	Wed 6th		5 Officers and 200 other Ranks employed on VAULX-MORCHIES line wiring under R.E. supervision. Remainder of battalion employed on improvement of camp.	
LAGNICOURT.	Thur 7th		Relieved 4th Bn. South Staffs Regt in the line. Relief commenced 6-30 p.m. finished 9 p.m. Night very dark. Enemy shelled spasmodically. 2 men wounded, 1 remaining at duty.	
"	Fri 8th		Dull & showery. Brig Gen. BAIRD left Bde for India - succeeded by Brig Gen DOBBIN - Enemy artillery fairly active.	
"	Sat 9th		Fine - but dull - Heavy enemy shelling on front line - also behind LAGNICOURT - Forward post on left of POULTRY - received direct hit about 1 am. - 1 killed, 1 wounded. One man also killed R Sub-sector 11 am. - Suspect new Regiment opposite.	
"	Sun 10th		Fine - intermittent shelling on QUEANT road - also a post hit during night - Met G.O.C. Div in RIPON ALLEY. [illegible] BIRT departed on long leave - Enemy active in [illegible]	
	Mon 11th		Representatives of relieving unit visited the line. Weather fine and trenches in good condition.	

28 N.

Instructions regarding War Diaries and Intelligence Summaries are contained in F. S. Regs., Part II. and the Staff Manual respectively. Title pages will be prepared in manuscript.

WAR DIARY
or
INTELLIGENCE SUMMARY.
(Erase heading not required.)

Army Form C. 2118.

Place	Date	Hour	Summary of Events and Information	Remarks and references to Appendices
LAGNICOURT.	Tues 12th		Battalion relieved in the line by 1st Bn K.S.L.I. and moved back to Camp No 16. Relief completed at 10.30 pm.	
LOGEAST CAMP	Wed 13th		Battalion moved back into Corps Reserve with remainder of Division. Took over ~~camp~~ LOGEAST CAMP. Rained practically all day.	
"	Thurs 14th		Major J. L. Wilkinson left to take over command of 11th Cheshires. Major T. Darwell MC took over command of battalion. Day spent in cleaning up kit &c.	
"	Fri 15th		Programme of training carried out preceded by half an hour ceremonial parade.	
"	Sat 16th		— do — — do — — do —	
"	Sun 17th		Divine Service. Recreational training in afternoon. Lieut Col C.W.H. Birt DSO rejoined battalion.	
"	Mon 18th		Major T. Darwell MC proceeded on leave to England. Programme of training carried out preceded by half an hour ceremonial parade.	
"	Tues 19th		Programme of training carried out preceded by half an hour ceremonial parade	
"	Wed 20th		— do — — do — — do —	
"	Thurs 21st		— do — — do — — do —	
"	Fri 22nd		— do — — do — — do —	
"	Sat 23rd		— do — — do — — do —	
"	Sun 24th		Divine Service. Recreational training in afternoon.	
"	Mon 25th		Programme of training carried out preceded by half an hour ceremonial parade	
"	Tues 26th		— do — — do — — do —	
"	Wed 27th		— do — — do — — do —	
"	Thurs 28th		— do — — do — — do —	

C.W.H. Birt
Lt Col

A7092). Wt. W12839/M.293 750,000. 1/17. D. D & L., Ltd. Forms/C2118/14.

25th Division.

75th Infantry Brigade.

WAR DIARY

8th BATTALION

THE BORDER REGIMENT

MARCH 1 9 1 8

Instructions regarding War Diaries and Intelligence Summaries are contained in F. S. Regs., Part II. and the Staff Manual respectively. Title pages will be prepared in manuscript.

WAR DIARY or ~~INTELLIGENCE SUMMARY.~~

(Erase heading not required.)

8th Border Regt 15/75

Army Form C. 2118.

MARCH 1918

Vol 30

Place	Date	Hour	Summary of Events and Information	Remarks and references to Appendices
LOGEAST CAMP ACHIET Area	Fri March 1st		Training Continued. Ceremonial Parade. Firing on 100 yards Range (15 rounds Rapid Fire and 5 rounds application with Box Respirators. Coy Training in Bombing, etc and Jump Lines. Remainder of Battalion (about 100) passed through Gas Chamber.	
	Sat 2nd		Training Continued. Firing on 30 yds Range. Coy Training. Surprise Gas Alarms. Demonstrations of PBT by selected platoon of H.A.C. at DIV HQRS. C.O. Officers and 45 OR's attended Lecture in Brigade Cinema on Growth of R.F.C. by O.C. 59th Squadron	
	Sun 3rd		Divine Services and Recreational Training. Officer's Record of Services Book received and issued, supplying a want much felt by junior officers owing to changes from one Battalion to another.	
	Mon 4th		Training Continued. Bde Horse Show on cold wintry afternoon. Cup for best Cooker won by 8th Borders, also 2nd & 3rd in limbers and 2nd in Mess Cart.	
	Tues 5th		Training Continued. Capt A.J. Bentley rejoined Battalion from Hospital and resumed command of C Coy. Intimation received that 2/Lt (T/Capt) J.G. Runciman Royal Scots attached this battalion had been posted to 5/6 Royal Scots. Night Firing on Corps Reinforcement Camp Range from 6.30pm to 10pm	
	Wed 6th		Training Continued. Commanding Officer took all officers over ground for proposed night Assembly and Attack. Weather mild and bright and Bde Sports took place in afternoon.	
	Thurs 7th		Training continued. Firing on 30 yds range. Night operations.	
	Fri 8th		Returned to camp from night operations 8 am. No training in morning. Lewis Gun Class &c in afternoon. D Coy on 200 yds range in afternoon.	29. N/ 5 sheets

A7092). Wt. W12839/M1293 750,000. 1/17. D. D & L., Ltd. Forms/C2118/14.

Army Form C. 2118.

Instructions regarding War Diaries and Intelligence Summaries are contained in F. S. Regs., Part II. and the Staff Manual respectively. Title pages will be prepared in manuscript.

WAR DIARY
or
INTELLIGENCE SUMMARY.
(Erase heading not required.)

Place	Date March 1918	Hour	Summary of Events and Information	Remarks and references to Appendices
LOGEAST CAMP	Sat 9th		Training continued. Firing on 300 yds range (15 rounds rapid & 5 rounds application). Recreational Training in afternoon.	
ACHIET AREA.	Sun 10th		Divine Service & recreational training.	
	Mon 11th		Training continued. Ceremonial parade. Musketry (15 rounds rapid). Brigade Staff Ride for Coy Commanders. Recreational Training.	
	Tues 12th		Training continued. Ceremonial parade. Musketry Recreational Training.	
SAVOY CAMP. ACHIET AREA.	Wed 13th		— do — Brigade removed to SAVOY CAMP.	
	Thurs 14th		~ do ~	
	Fri 15th		~ do ~	
	Sat 16th		~ do ~	
	Sun 17th		Divine Service & Recreational Training.	
	Mon 18th		Training continued. Ceremonial parade. Musketry. Recreational Training.	
	Tues 19th		Training continued. Ceremonial parade. Recreational Training. Practice attack under Brigade arrangements.	
	Wed 20th		Training continued. Musketry. Lewis gun classes. Recreational Training.	

A7092). Wt. W12839/M1293 750,000. 1/17. D. D & L., Ltd. Forms/C2118/14.

WAR DIARY
or
INTELLIGENCE SUMMARY.
(*Erase heading not required.*)

Army Form C. 2118.

Instructions regarding War Diaries and Intelligence Summaries are contained in F. S. Regs., Part II. and the Staff Manual respectively. Title pages will be prepared in manuscript.

March 1918

Place	Date	Hour	Summary of Events and Information	Remarks and references to Appendices
SAVOY CAMP ACHIET AREA	21st		Heavy gun fire 5.30 am – Bn stood to 7.00 am – Bn moved off 9.10 am under Lt Col Birt – with 1st line T'port to 150 Labour Coy Camp at BEUGNATRE – Bn was placed under orders of 16th Bde – & was ordered to Counter attack North of VAULX Wood in the VAULX-MORCHIES line. Capt Hore killed after leaving BEUGNATRE – Order of Battle from Right – A Coy (Capt BIRNIE), B Coy (Lt REED), C Coy (Lt ALLAN) with D Coy (Lt DUGGAN) in reserve – Counter attack reached 1st objective 3.10 pm – & did not proceed further owing to wire being uncut. Communication established on the right by Lt BELL & party – D Coy filled gap on left – forming up with BUFFS on Rt & RSF on left. Lt REED killed in VAULX-MORCHIES line & died of wounds.	
VAULX-MORCHIES line	22nd		Shelling began early & enemy attacked about 7.30 am – & penetrated VAULX WOOD on our right – The Bn was surrounded on 3 sides – & for 4 hours under Capt BIRNIE – held the enemy at bay – & only withdrew at 1 pm – our right being in the air – & the Divn on our left falling back – All communication with Artillery & Bde was cut – Bn withdrew to VAULX-FREMICOURT Road. During the day Lts DOWDELL, McTAVISH, & WARWICK were killed – The Bn eventually reorganized in ARMY LINE assisted by Scotch troops (51st Divn) Bn relieved by 41st Divn – 4 Capt Lt GARDEN, Lt FENTIMAN, & 24 OR who refused to leave until properly relief – which never came. 2/Lt FRYER missing. CAPT BIRNIE, Lts GANDOLFO 2/Lt LIGHTFOOT, & SANDWELL wounded.	
SAVOY CAMP	23rd		Bn relieved & moved to SAVOY CAMP – hot meal at 4 am – At 9 am ordered to move to ridge E of BEHAGNIES-SAPIGNIES road & dig in – About 4 pm – B echelon from 25 ORS under MAJOR WILKINSON & 140 OR – arrived – & Lt Col BIRT handed over command & went down to Transport	
BEHAGNIES SAPIGNIES Road	24th		Trenches improved during day. Shelling became active in afternoon & increased – Situation became very vague – & Lt ALLAN twice went forward to report – Night passed without incident – Bn was relieved by 1 Coy 5th Lancs Fusiliers (42nd Divn) & moved to	
LOGEAST WOOD	25th		LOGEAST WOOD – where the Bn dug in E of wood – Lt Col BIRT resumed command – Shelling was intermittent but never very heavy – Orders received 8 pm to move to PUISIEUX AU MONT	
PUISIEUX AU MONT	26th		Dug in – PUISIEUX – with 62 Divn on left – Information received 4 am that enemy held MIRAUMONT & that our R flank was in the air & orders were received to concentrate north of GOMMECOURT – which was reached 6.30 am – At 10 am moved to form defensive flank SE of GOMMECOURT & then withdrawn to rest – MAJOR WILKINSON rejoined & took over command – took up defensive position N of GOMMECOURT – 7th & 74th Bde in front – 75th in support – At midnight Bn was relieved & moved to	Division
COIGN	27th		COIGN – arriving 4 am – where a good night's sleep was obtained – left 3.30 pm & marched to	
PUCHEVILLERS	28th		PUCHEVILLERS arriving 8 pm – & left next morning 7.30 am for	
VACQUERIE	29th		VACQUERIE arriving about 2 pm – & billeted there	
do	30th		Cleaning up & refitting	
do	31st		Marched to DOULLENS & entrained for GODEWAERSVELDE	

W N Birt Lt Col
Commanding, 8th (S) Bn The Border Regt

25th Division

75th Infantry Brigade.

WAR DIARY

8th BATTALION

THE BORDER REGIMENT

APRIL 1918

Report on Operations 3rd to 19th April 1918

Instructions regarding War Diaries and Intelligence Summaries are contained in F. S. Regs., Part II. and the Staff Manual respectively. Title pages will be prepared in manuscript.

WAR DIARY
or
INTELLIGENCE SUMMARY.
(Erase heading not required.)

8th Border Regt.

Army Form C. 2118.

75/75

Vol 31

April 1918

Place	Date	Hour	Summary of Events and Information	Remarks and references to Appendices
[G]ODEWAERSVELDE [K]ORTEPYP CAMP	April 1st – M		Advance Coy D Coy arrived 1.30 am + remainder of Bn 5 am + Embussed for KORTEPYP CAMP – New draft of 170 19 year old boys – Excellent appearance + smart of parade – CAPT. I DAWSON rejoined	
[RO]MARIN CAMP	2nd Tues		Moved to ROMARIN CAMP – 2nd S Lancs in line – 8 Border support, 11th Cheshire reserve – D Coy – under Capt DAWSON (Lancashire Support FARM). Counter attacking Coy – under tactical orders of 7S Lancs – C Coy CAPT BENTLEY A + B Coys, ROMARIN CAMP with Bn HQrs – Brilliant weather	
	3rd Wed		Cleaning up – + baths – Unsettled	
	4th Thur		Unsettled – Cleaning up – + inspections – C + D Coys withdrawn from Support line – preparatory to moving up next day – OC Coys reconnoitred front line. 5th	
TOUQUET Sector	5th Fri		Bn relieved 3rd Lancashire + 11th Lancs Fusiliers – Bn sector Lys River on right to Cub 7.8 on left – C Coy (Capt Bentley) Left Subsector, D Coy (Capt Dawson) Right Subsector B Coy – Support – Grande Rabecque – A Coy – Reserve – Le Bizet – Bn HQrs Desquesne Farm – Relief began 7.30 pm + finished 10 pm – Capt Sports D Coy 3 am. Night wet	
	6. Sat.		Fine, CO visited OC front line Coys. C + D – Day quiet. Patrols out at night	
	7 Sun		Routine in the Line. A little TM activity. Persistent firing by enemy MG all night from FRELINGHEIN	
	8 Mon.		do. Fairly quiet MG fired from FRELINGHEIN all night. Patrol located strong enemy working party at West end of FRELINGHEIN BRIDGE. They were wiring the Bridge Head. 2nd S Lancs on our left relieved by XI Cheshires. A Coy (2/Lt Allan) moved up from LE BIZET to GRANDE RABEQUE. B Coy side slipping to the right in the RESERVE LINE. Enemy TMS in WARNETON Sector heavily bombarded during the afternoon.	
	9 Tues		Dull + cloudy. Heavy bombardment on our right – several miles away. Reported GERMAN attack from ARMENTIERES to LA BASSEE. Our Sector heavily shelled in afternoon – with Gas – HE + Shrapnel. A Coy (2/Lt ALLAN) relieved C Coy (Capt BENTLEY) in left front. B Coy (Capt COXON) relieved D Coy (Capt. DAWSON) in right front.	
	10 Wed		Dull – slight mist. Enemy attacked about 5.30 am after a heavy bombardment. A Coy practically cut off. B.C + D Coys retired to Reserve Line – which was soon enveloped. + about mid-day Battalion withdrew with other troops to a NORTH and SOUTH Line West of LE BIZET. A further withdrawal to the ROAD Clef de la BELGIQUE — OOSTHOVE was necessitated during the afternoon, and late at night the right flank was swung back to the line COURTE RUE OOSTHOVE – DOUDOU – Two Companies 9th Cheshires being on our right at COURTE RUE and 2 Companies 9th Cheshires on our left at OOSTHOVE.	80.N.

A7092). Wt. W12839/M1293 750,000. 1/17. D. D & L., Ltd. Forms/C2118/14.

WAR DIARY
or
INTELLIGENCE SUMMARY.
(Erase heading not required.)

Army Form C. 2118.

Instructions regarding War Diaries and Intelligence Summaries are contained in F. S. Regs., Part II. and the Staff Manual respectively. Title pages will be prepared in manuscript.

Place	Date 1918	Hour	Summary of Events and Information	Remarks and references to Appendices
T HOVE ME ROSSIGNOL	Apl 11 Thurs		Enemy attacked early morning but was driven off by rifle & LG fire. Position bombarded fairly heavily. About midday a withdrawal on the left necessitated falling back on TRENCH LINE about LE ROSSIGNOL, which was held till night. Lt STRONG & party of 40. O.R. captured a MG & restored a temporary gap in the line about BRUNE GAYE in the afternoon. Orders to evacuate NIEPPE SALIENT being received, the Battalion withdrew to CONNAUGHT ROAD at dusk – where it dug in in support to 75th Inf Bde Group.	
NAUGHT OAD TE PYP.	Apl 12. Fri		Day was fine. Beyond little shelling & sniping nothing of great importance occurred during the morning. About 2pm a general retirement was observed on our right – which necessitated a further withdrawal to KORTE PYP. – where the line was reorganised.	
VE GLISE	13 Sat		Very heavy mist in morning. The night had passed quietly. About 6am 6th SWB were seen to be retiring along the NEUVE EGLISE Road & soon after under cover of mist & the heavy bombardment enemy attacked in great strength & forced us back to the line NEUVE EGLISE – TROIS ROIS CABT where elements of 75th Bde Group & the 9th H.L.I. had already dug in. Here a stand was made. Capt COXON & Lt BOTT were both killed making a counter attack on the enemy's flank during the morning. Meantime a position was being prepared from CRUCIFIX CORNER along the ridge in a NORTH EASTERLY direction	
	14. Sun		Morning quiet except for heavy shelling of back areas. About midday enemy began dribbling small parties forward & soon evidence of massing was observed in the valley along the NEUVE EGLISE ~~Road~~ – DRANOUTRE ROAD about T8c Central. Our barrage & MG fire nipped the attack in the bud. Orders for Bde relief received about 9.30pm	
DOKOT ES CATS.	15 Mon		Battalion relieved in line by ~~15~~ 71st Bde about 2.30 am & marched to KOUDOKOT where it joined the rest of the Brigade. At 2pm the Brigade marched via BERTHEN to MONT DES CATS which was reached about 7pm.	

A7092). Wt. W12839/M1293 750,000. 1/17. D. D & L., Ltd. Forms/C2118/14.

Instructions regarding War Diaries and Intelligence Summaries are contained in F. S. Regs., Part II. and the Staff Manual respectively. Title pages will be prepared in manuscript.

WAR DIARY
or
INTELLIGENCE SUMMARY.
(Erase heading not required.)

Army Form C. 2118.

Place	Date 1918 Apl	Hour	Summary of Events and Information	Remarks and references to Appendices
[LA L]EVRETTE	16 Tues.		About 10.45pm Battalion marched via BOESCHEPE to LALEVRETTE in support to 33rd & 34th Divisions. Bde formed into a composite Battalion under Lt Col J. B. ALLSOPP. Capt BENTLEY and Lt DUGGAN remained with Battalion. Lt Col BIRT returned to rear Brigade H.Q.	
	17 Wed.		Still at LALEVRETTE – Shelled rather heavily during the day.	
[MONT DE]S CATS	18 Thurs		Early morning the Battalion returned to Hutments at MONT DES CATS. Major STEWART rejoined the Battalion temporarily in the evening. Draft of young boys mostly.	
	19 Frid		Snow fell – very cold. Shell burst in C Coys hut killing 5 & wounding 26 O.R.	
	20 Sat		Cold. Cleaning up & refitting. Enemy shelled vicinity fairly heavily. Classes for Specialists. Firing on range behind MONASTRY. Inlying picquet established and safeguard against surprise.	
[VO]X VRIE [POPE]RINGHE	21 Sun		Brigade marched to HIRST CAMP near VOX VRIE – POPERINGHE. Fine.	
	22 Mond		Fine. Classes continued. 18 officers joined Battalion in afternoon & draft of 63 O.R.	
	23 Tues		Lewis Gun Classes continued. 2nd Lt. MACKIE joined the Bn and was posted to A Co.	
	24 Wed		Specialists Classes continued. Lt M TURNBULL joined the Bn. He was posted to D. Co and appointed Bn Signalling officer.	
	25 Thur		The Bn was employed in digging trench line.	
	~~26 Fri~~		At 10 A.M. orders were issued from Bde warning the Bn to stand by ready to move. Coys were recalled from digging and preparations made for an immediate move. At 2.30pm the Brigade moved to	

Instructions regarding War Diaries and Intelligence Summaries are contained in F. S. Regs., Part II. and the Staff Manual respectively. Title pages will be prepared in manuscript.

WAR DIARY
or
INTELLIGENCE SUMMARY.
(*Erase heading not required.*)

Army Form C. 2118.

Place	Date April 1918.	Hour	Summary of Events and Information	Remarks and references to Appendices
HOUGRAAF CABARET.	25 Thur		to HOUGRAAF CABARET where the Division were ordered to Concentrate at 11 pm the Division received orders to Counter attack in the vicinity of KEMMEL. The 7th Brigade on the right and the 74th Brigade on the left were ordered to move forward in conjunction with the 39th French Division. The 75th Bde were in close support. The Battalion moved forward and took up a position on the right of the LA. CLYTTE – RENINGHELST road about 600 yds E of RENINGHELST at	
RENINGHELST.	26 Fri		2 AM. Owing to heavy Enemy shelling D. Coy. [illegible] to a new position on the flank. The remainder of the day was fairly quiet.	
NE	27 Sat		During the afternoon the Bn moved forward and relieved the 10th Cheshires (7th Brigade) In the evening the Bn moved into the front line and relieved 8th Loyal North Lancs and 3rd Worcesters. Patrols were sent out during the night. Small parties of the Enemy were encountered and dispersed	
	28 Sun.		Intermittent hostile shelling throughout the day. Otherwise quiet. Lt. F. W. DARVELL took out a patrol during the day and patrolled the whole of the right front. During the night patrols were again sent out and a little wiring was done.	
	29 Mon		at 3 AM. the Enemy opened a bombardment of Gas Shells which at 5 AM developed into a heavy HE barrage. The S.O.S. was seen going up on the left of the line	

A7092). Wt. W12839/M1293 750,000. 1/17. D. D & L., Ltd. Forms/C2118/14.

Instructions regarding War Diaries and Intelligence Summaries are contained in F. S. Regs., Part II. and the Staff Manual respectively. Title pages will be prepared in manuscript.

WAR DIARY
or
INTELLIGENCE SUMMARY.
(Erase heading not required.)

Army Form C. 2118.

Place	Date April 1918	Hour	Summary of Events and Information	Remarks and references to Appendices
[illegible]NE.	29. Mon.		At 6.15 AM The two front Cos reported that the Enemy were massing on the right front and appeared to be attempting to attack down the LA CLYTTE – KEMMIL road. Owing to our Artillery, MG and rifle fire the attack did not develop. About this time the two front Cos were subjected to heavy MG and rifle fire from the right front. At 10 AM. Lt Col C W. H. BIRT. DSO was wounded in the left arm by a shell. Capt A J. BENTLEY A/adjt took over Command of the Bn.	
			Up to 11 AM Considerable enemy movement was observed on the right front. MG and rifle fire was opened on them and heavy casualties inflicted.	
			Owing to heavy hostile shelling throughout the morning Communication with the rear was difficult.	
			At 5.15 pm. the Enemy opened a heavy barrage on our Front and Support which Continued until 6.15 pm when the Enemy again appeared to be attempting to attack along the LA CLYTTE – KEMMIL road. This attack was again broken up by Artillery. MG and rifle fire. The remainder of the day was without incident. The following officers were wounded during the morning.	
			CAPT C. W. McLENNAN. Gassed went down to ADS and returned to the Bn.	
			2 Lts. J. W ROGERS (B Co) J. GIBSON (B Co) J. T. R VAREL (B Co) J. H. MACKIE (A Co)	
			On the night of 29/30 the Bn was relieved by 2nd Bn South Lancs.	

A7092). Wt. W12839/M1293 750,000. 1/17. D. D. & L., Ltd. Forms/C2118/14.

Army Form C. 2118.

WAR DIARY
or
INTELLIGENCE SUMMARY.
(Erase heading not required.)

Instructions regarding War Diaries and Intelligence Summaries are contained in F. S. Regs., Part II. and the Staff Manual respectively. Title pages will be prepared in manuscript.

Place	Date April 1918.	Hour	Summary of Events and Information	Remarks and references to Appendices
LINE	29 Mon.		On relief the Bn. moved back to a position on the LA-CLYTTE–RENINGHELST road 800 yds west of LA CLYTTE. Here Major. H.G FRASER joined the Bn. and assumed Command.	
[illegible] CLYTTE.	30 [illegible]		The day was fairly quiet. At 6 pm. the vicinity of Bn. HQ was heavily shelled for about an hour.	
			Honours and Awards during Month.	
			32272. Cpl. J. S. SEWELL; 12235 " J. W. BURKIN; 9844 " P. CARR; 24645 L/C F. LEE; 11884 Sjt J. MACDONALD; 21036 Cpl H. WISE; 27434 Pte. H. SINGLETON; 5622 " H. FERGUSON; 18388 Pte R. LAWRENCE; 13589 " J. VARITY; 16233 L/C B. DUCKWORTH; 30198 Pte G. PORTER; 15597 L/C G. JOHNSTON; 14509 Pte. J. KELLY; 15091. Sjt M. CRAYSTON. — MILITARY MEDAL for Conspicuous gallantry during the retreat on the SOMME.	

[signature] Capt
for Major Commdg.
8th Bn. The Border Regt.

A7092). Wt. W12839/M1293 750,000. 1/17. D. D & L., Ltd. Forms/C2118/14.

Apr 3rd 1918 to Apr 19th 1918

KORTEPYP-ROMARIN 3.IV.18 The Battalion arrived at GODEWAERSVELDE early in the morning of Apr. 1st (Easter Monday) and proceeded by lorry to KORTEPYP CAMP. Here reorganisation was proceeded with and on the 2nd and 3rd reinforcements arrived - including Capt. J. DAWSON M.C who had been wounded at MESSINES in June 1917. Among the reinforcements were some 200 youths of the age of 18 or 19 - a very smart lot and who later did wonderfully well in action.

On the 2nd Apr. reconnaissance of the Support Lines in the PLOEGSTEERT Sector was made by Capts. BENTLEY & DAWSON and officers of C and D Coys. These two companies moved up to certain posts in support of 2nd STH. LANCS. on the night 3/4th April

ROMARIN 4.IV.18 Intimation having been received that the Battalion was to take over from two Battalions of 74th BDE on the following night in the LETOUQUET Sector the C.O. received permission to withdraw these 2 Coys from the Support Line - which was done during the day and evening. The C.O. attended at 74th BDE H.Q. during the afternoon where arrangements were made for the relief of 3rd WORCESTERS and 11th LANC FUS. on the following night.

5.IV.18 In the morning Officers and N.C.Os. from each Coy proceeded to LETOUQUET Sector to reconnoitre the line and in the evening the Battalion relieved the 2 Battalions of 74th BDE in the line as under.-

BATLN. H.Q - DESPIERRE FARM

C.O.	Lt Col	C.W.H. BIRT D.S.O
2nd in C.	Maj	T.S. WILKINSON
ADJT	2/Lt.	J. GRELLIS M.C
SIGNALS	Lt.	G.G.R. BOTT M.C
LEWIS GUN	Lt.	R. STRONG M.C.
INT. OFF	2/Lt	T. VAUGHAN
R.S.M		LIGHTFOOT M.C. DCM

"D" Coy RIGHT FRONT

Capt	J. DAWSON M.C
Lt	J. DUGGAN D.C.M
2/Lt	F.C. CORLEY
-	H.T. LAY
-	G.F. HOOK
C.S.M	E. WAUGH D.C.M

"C" Coy. LEFT FRONT

Capt	A.J. BENTLEY
2/Lt	W.J. CROOKSTON
-	T.F. MIDDLETON
C.S.M	J. DAWSON

"B" Coy SUPPORT (GRANDE RABECQUE)

Capt	P.H. COXON MC
Lt	M.C. CLODD
2/Lt	A.B. CAMERON M.M
C.S.M	E. HIGHAM D.C.M

LE TOUQUET
5/9. iv. 18

"A" Coy 2nd Lt. J. W. A. ALLAN
RESERVE — W. C. PRESTON
LE BIZET — C. A. WATTS
C.S.M. J. GENT

The Sector was a comparatively quiet one and during the period 6th, 7th & 8th Apr. nothing of great moment was detected.

An incident worthy of record is that each night a M.G. in the village of FRELINGHEIN kept up an incessant fire from dusk to dawn. Bullets fell in the region of DESPIERRE and SEVEN TREES AVENUE. It was deduced that the object of this M.G. fire was not to harass our lines but rather to cover the noise made by enemy working parties.

During the period 6th to 8th work was carried on and patrols sent out each night. On the night 7/8th April a strong enemy working party was detected at west end of FRELINGHEIN Bridge, and the patrol after investigating reported wiring in progress across the Bridgehead.

Early morning of 9th April heavy gunfire on the right heralded the opening of enemy offensive from LABASSEE to ARMENTIERES. A strict watch was accordingly kept for any signs of unusual movement upon our front. During the afternoon the enemy heavily bombarded our back areas, gas shell being used, and later our front line received attention from the enemy's guns and TMs., but as little damage resulted it was not thought that any special operations were impending.

9. iv. 18 During the night "A" Coy. relieved "C" in the front, and "B" relieved "D" on right front – "C" and "D" moving back to reserve line – LYS FARM – GUNNERS FARM.

Three patrols were sent out along the river – one each from "A" "B" & "D" Coys. The former did not return, but nil reports were received from the two latter.

LE TOUQUET OOSTHOVE 10. iv. 18 Lt. BOTT M.C., ably assisted by Sgt. J GRANT D.C.M. had established telephonic communication with all Coys. and with outlying posts, and during the early hours BATTN. H.Q. was in almost constant communication with all Companies. Beyond the heavy bombardment nothing extraordinary was reported. As late as 6 a.m. "A" Coy. (left front) reported "All well" but soon after a message was received from Capt COXON ("B" Coy) that the enemy were in HALFWAY HOUSE, and a little later at LE TOUQUET STA. Capt COXON reported that he was compelled to withdraw to RAILWAY SWITCH, several of his posts having been cut off. Nothing more was heard from "A" Coy. tho later it transpired that 2nd Lt. PRESTON, CSM GENT and about 20 O.R. had been driven back towards PLOEGSTEERT WOOD where a junction was effected with remnants of the 7th Brigade. It is presumed that the remainder of "A" Coy were cut off – Mr ALLAN being badly wounded. Mr WATTS was also wounded, but managed to escape.

LE TOUQUET OOSTHOVE 10. IV. 18 Both Support Coys. having been warned to be ready for immediate action a watch was set from BATT. HQ. to endeavour to discover what the real situation was - all spare rifles being sent down NICHOLSON AVENUE to keep in touch with Support Coys. in the Reserve Line.

At 6.45 a.m. the watch reported that BATT. HQ. was being outflanked from the direction of SURREY FARM and also from the direction of RESERVE FARM - indeed by that time H.Q. was already cut off from front and rear and there was nothing else for it but to fall back and endeavour to either

(a) get in touch with XI CHESHIRES or (b) work around to LE BIZET and rejoin the Support Coys.

As it happened the XI CHESHIRES appeared to be in much the same plight, and it was only by making a considerable detour around the north end of PLOEGSTEERT VILLAGE that the C.O. and his orderly were able to get around the enemy and rejoin the remainder of the Battalion in the Reserve Line. Even then enemy M.G. fire was opened from a house in the village.

LE BIZET OOSTHOVE 10. IV. 18

Meanwhile "B", "C" & "D" Coys. under Captns. COXON, BENTLEY, and DAWSON were still holding out in the Line GUNNERS FARM - LYS FARM, and as Companies of the 2nd Sth. LANCS and 6th. S.W.B had been sent up to their assistance - the position was not devoid of hope as the 34th. Division (South of the LYS) were still in the line and had not been attacked. This was the position when about 9 a.m. the C.O. rejoined the Battalion. Unfortunately our left flank in NICHOLSON AVEN (GUNNERS FARM) though it had touched up with a post of the XI CHESHIRES was otherwise in the air - the enemy holding TILLEUL just NORTH WEST of GUNNERS FARM. More unfortunately still the S.W.Bs. at this time were withdrawn to DOU - DOU FARM and the chance to extend our left flank was missed. Having sized up the situation and sending word to Capt. DAWSON as to the danger on the left flank, the C.O. proceeded to report to BRIG. GEN. HANNAY (who had relieved GEN DOBBIN the day previous). Returning to LE BIZET it was seen that the enemy had enveloped our left flank by moving on GASOMETER CORNER on the north end of LE BIZET. No counter attacking troops being available a withdrawal was necessary. This was only achieved with difficulty - Lt. DUGGAN and a party of "D" Coy. found it necessary to rush GRANDE RABECQUE and the north end of LE BIZET - capturing a M.G. in doing so. Having no ammunition for the gun it was thrown into the bottom of a ditch. By 1 p.m. the withdrawal was well underway and the line was reorganised just WEST of LE BIZET as under:-

LE BIZET R.E's. Capt. CATON (?)
D-B-C Coys. BORDERS.
1 Coy S.W.B's.
1 - 2nd S. LANCS MAJOR STEWART
joining up with 2 Companies of 9th CHESHIRES (COL FULTON) who in turn joined up with remnants of XI CHESHIRES

LE BIZET
OOSTHOVE
10. IV. 18

BORDERS, 2nd S. LANCS under LT. COL. J. B. ALLSOPP at REGINA FARM. The right flank of this line was resting on the LYS and 2 Companies of 9th CHESHIRES were in support on the OOSTHOVE Road.

Early in the afternoon MAJOR BELLINGHAM (M.G. Battn) reported that one Company of 2nd STH. LANCS. under CAPT. ROSS was still east of LE BIZET. An attempt was made to join up with this Company across the North end of LE BIZET thus in the hope of still keeping touch with the 34th Division who were holding the RAILWAY BRIDGE with a M.G. A patrol under LT. J. DUGGAN was accordingly sent out by CAPT DAWSON but LE BIZET was found to be strongly held with M.G's. and as by this time the Coy. of 2nd STH. LANCS. were retiring the project was abandoned. About 1 p.m. LT. BOTT and MAJ. WILKINSON rejoined the Battalion having attached themselves to LT. COL. ALLSOPP'S party earlier in the day. 2nd LT. GRELLIS and R.S.M. LIGHTFOOT remaining with a detail of about 100 men of the BORDERS who had come up from TRANSPORT. Acting under orders of G.O.C. DIVISION LT COL ALLSOPP'S party at 5.30 p.m. counter-attacked the village of PLOEGSTEERT - the right of the line being ordered to conform with his advance. Unfortunately word did not reach the right until 6.10 p.m. and it was then too late to take any part in the counter attack - which was not successful owing to the extraordinary number of M.G's. which the enemy had placed in the several farm-houses along his front. Enemy M.G's. had also been placed in the southern end of LE BIZET. At about 6.30 p.m the extreme right flank was seen to retire and also some S.W.B's. in the Centre. This was followed by a general withdrawal of the right on to the OOSTHOVE ROAD. It is not definitely known why this retirement took place, as nowhere was the enemy pressing. The withdrawal was a costly one owing to the heavy M.G. fire over the very flat stretch of country. Elements of the Brigade who had fallen back were reorganised in front of the road running South from OOSTHOVE and continuing on to the River LYS - the R.Es. being on the right, BORDERS next touching up with 9th CHESHIRES on our left. The night was exceedingly quiet and there was almost an entire lack of artillery fire on both sides.

Communication was by runner – no other being available.
During the night orders were received to swing our
right flank back so as to face South – 9TH. CHESHIRES to
be on right in touch with COURTE RUE, the BORDERS on
their left with their right flank in OOSTHOVE –
11. IV. 18 touching up with the other two Companies 9th CHESH. who
in turn were in touch with S.W.Bs. on the line EAST of
OOSTHOVE - DOU - DOU. This movement was carried into
effect about 2 a.m. and completed just before dawn.
BORDERS were formed in following order from the right –
B-C-D Coys, very few of A Coy being with us at the time,
tho. some rejoined under C.S.M. GENT later. Soon after
daylight the enemy began shelling our positions with
OOSTHOVE guns and TMs, and strong parties were observed moving
11. IV. 18. forward to the attack, but were dispersed by our L.G. and
rifle fire.
The morning was cold with little rain, but visibility was fair.
Aircraft (both ours and enemy's) flew close over our position.
One of ours was brought down by enemy rifle fire, and
soon after an enemy plane flying low over "B" Coy's.
position was brought to earth by the fire from that Company.
This was the second enemy plane to our Battalion credit
in two days. The day previous one came down with
engine trouble and was just starting off again when
it was rushed by Ptes. 14659 WILLIAM STAFFORD,
15047 JAMES GEORGE, 15754 THOMAS McGUINNESS who,
wounding the observer, succeeded in capturing the plane.
About MIDDAY parties of the S.W.B on our left having
fallen back on to the trench line running along the
EAST of ROMARIN it was necessary to conform to the
movement, and accordingly the two left Companies
of 9th CHESHIRES and the 8th BORDERS were withdrawn
fighting to the trench line. Two companies 9th CHESHIRES
touched up with 1/7th DUKE OF WELLINGTONS at COURTE RUE
ROSSIGNOL BORDERS were on their left, touching up with the remaining
11. IV. 18 two Companies 9th CHESHIRES whose left extended up
towards BRUNE GAY. Our position was quite secure to the
front, but early in the afternoon an enemy M.G
firing from WEST OF ROMARIN caused much uneasiness,
especially as there was always danger of being cut
off in the neck of the NIEPPE SALIENT. Precautions
for a possible retirement were taken. LT. COL. FULTON
Cdg. 9th CHESHIRES investigated the matter and located
the M.G. A party of 30 BORDERS and 10 CHESHIRES
(40 all told) under LT. R. STRONG M.C. proceeded to
restore the situation, and about 3 p.m. a report was
received from LT. STRONG to the effect that he had
captured the M.G. and 1 Off and 8 O.R. prisoners and was holding
the gap in the line EAST of BRUNE GAY.

ROSSIGNOL 11. IV. 18 Unfortunately LT. STRONG was wounded and an officer of 9th CHESHIRES took charge. About an hour later we were again disturbed by an 18 pdr. (BRITISH) firing with open sights from the direction of ROMARIN into our backs. Fortunately no one was hit and word was sent asking the gunners to lift 500 yards. But the gun proved to have been a captured one fired by the enemy and precautions for a withdrawal were again taken. At 7.30 p.m. orders were received to evacuate the NIEPPE SALIENT and acting in conjunction with Lt COL. FULTON at 8.25 p.m. the Battalion withdrew to the Support taking up a position behind 11th CHESHIRES and

CONNAUGHT ROAD 11. IV. 18 6th S.W.B at CONNAUGHT ROAD. On the right about PAPOT were the MONMOUTHS (88th Bde). Touching their left were 9th CHESHIRES at LIMPERNESSE, then 11th CHESHIRES, 6th S.W.B, 2nd Sth LANCS in that order touching up with 16th KRRC (Lt COL JOHNSON) who were in the trench line NORTH of ROMARIN. Here we dug in in Support and the night passed quietly enough.

12. IV. 18 Early in the morning the enemy crumped the front line, but little damage was done. He soon occupied RUE DE SAC from which place he sniped and machine gunned continuously. He shelled back areas a great deal. Quite early our own heavies dropped short on our own lines, but this was fortunately soon rectified. Late in the morning MAJOR PRIOR sent word that the MONMOUTHS were being hard pressed about PONT D'ACHELLE and at about 2 p.m. a general retirement was observed on the right. For a while the situation was serious but KORTEPYP CAMP served as a good rallying point and here we very soon reorganised the whole Bde Group. 28895 Pte. WILLIAM HEWITT of A Coy with his Lewis Gun did splendid work here, very quickly dispersing two enemy M.G. teams. The line was reorganised as under:-

16th K.R.R.S at LEINSTER RD.
2nd STH. LANCS (+ Coy) CAPT ECKENSTEIN
11th CHESHIRES (MAJOR PRIOR)
8th BORDERS - B.C.D. Coys.
Details 16th K.R.R.S
6th S.W.B (COL. FITZPATRICK) who touched up with some of 88th Bde. on their right

Ammunition having been located in KORTEPYP it was distributed under the control of C.S.M. J.M. GENT and Sgt R.F. GRAHAM and all ranks and L.G.s were plentifully supplied with S.A.A and bombs. Posts were organised and patrols sent out at night which passed quietly.

13. IV. 18 A very heavy mist laying over the land at dawn. Under cover of this the enemy massed in front of our position. As early as 6 a.m. word was received that the S.W.Bs. were seen marching towards NEUVE EGLISE

13/IV/18 NEUVE EGLISE

Investigation confirmed this report and the H.Q. of 8 BORDERS together with some K.R.R.S were formed up to fill the breach. These were placed under the orders of MAJOR T.S. WILKINSON who had been untiring in his devotion to DUTY. He was soon after wounded and Lt. BOTT took charge of the party. Before they could fill the breach however the enemy had pressed back our right flank and by means of a hurricane bombardment of our line of posts we were compelled to withdraw towards NEUVE EGLISE. Our losses at KORTEPYP included Lt. CORLEY and C.S.M. E. WAUGH killed and CAPT. DAWSON and Lt. H.T. LAY wounded, Lt. VAUGHAN being wounded the day previous.

Elements of Bde Group were with the 9th H.L.I. entrenched on the HILLSIDE SPUR from AUTROIS ROIS CABT towards NEUVE EGLISE and here another stand was made. Quite early we were fired on by our own Artillery, but fortunately only for a short while. About 40 men of the Borders were collected on the right of the H.L.I. about TROIS ROIS CABT. With these were Capts COXON and BENTLEY and Lt. BOTT and Lt. CLODD and C.S.M. GENT. About 10 a.m. the enemy attacked the position on the left. It was observed that the left flank (opposite our right) of the enemy was wavering and a counter attack was immediately organised by Lt. BOTT and led by CAPT. COXON. He succeeded in causing great discomfiture to the now retiring enemy. Unfortunately this counter attack was not pushed far enough, and seeing it stop two enemy machine guns immediately turned on to the party. They took refuge in a drain and in trying to snipe the enemy machine Gunners both CAPT. COXON and Lt. BOTT and Sgt. J. GRANT were killed. L/Corporal BRAY of B Coy. did a splendid thing here. He rushed back through the M.G. fire, secured a Lewis Gun and, taking it to our left flank, opened fire on the M.Gs. Under cover of the L.G. fire the remainder of the party were successfully withdrawn.

Both CAPT. COXON and Lt. BOTT had done splendid work up to this and their death was a great loss. Sgt. J. GRANT (SIGNALS) had worked untiringly. He was a splendid example of BRITISH N.C.O.

For the remainder of the day the defence of HILLSIDE CAMP was devoid of incidents.

Meantime, a line had been organised along the ridge NORTH WEST of NEUVE EGLISE and was manned by parties of 7th Bde., 9th CHESHIRES, 6th S.W.B., 8th BORDERS and 16th K.R.R.C. to which the troops in front were able to retire when at last driven from HILLSIDE. The remaining officers of the Battalion - Lt. COL. BIRT, CAPT BENTLEY and Lt. DUGGAN collected about 126 men of the 8th BORDERS and arrangements were made for the defence of this position. The night passed without further incident.

NEUVE EGLISE 14.IV.18 The morning was quiet except for slight shelling of our front and heavy shelling of back areas. Little was known of the exact position on our front. Just before midday, however, Germans were seen moving from cover to cover, singly, and in what appeared to be more or less without object. No definite targets showed up, but after watching for some time it was seen that the enemy were really trickling forward M/Gs to cover their left flank for massing troops for an attack on the NEUVE EGLISE - DRANOUTRE Road where it crossed our line. M.G. and L.G. fire was opened and later the Artillery called on for a Barrage. Visual Signals had been organised with the Guns by L/C TANNAHILL and Pte. ROBERTS and the Barrage was thus so controlled that any projected attack was nipped in the bud, tho the enemy still maintained his forward position. Our casualties were negligable.

15.IV.18 At 9.30 p.m. orders for the relief of the 75th Bde Group by the 71st Bde. were received and at 2.30 a.m. relief being complete the Battalion marched back to KOUDOKOT, where the remainder of the Brigade were assembled. At 2 p.m. a move was made via MONT NOIR and BERTHEN for BOESCHEPE, but later the destination was altered to the HUTMENTS & BILLETS in the MONT DES CATS area.

16.IV.18 MONT DES CATS / LA LEVRETTE Our night's rest was much appreciated, but at 10.45 a.m. we were again on the move - this time in support behind the junction of 33rd and 34th Division at about LA LEVRETTE. The Battalion marched via BOESCHEPE, but when near Mt KOKEREELE it was decided to form the Brigade into a Composite Battalion under the Command of Lt COL J.B. ALLSOP (82nd Regt) - Lt COL BIRT returning to rear H.Q at BOESCHEPE. CAPT BENTLEY and Lt DUGGAN remained with the Battalion, but during the night 2/Lt PUGH was sent up to the relief of CAPT. BENTLEY who returned to Transport.
The stay at LA LEVRETTE was without incident, except for some heavy shelling which unfortunately caused several casualties.

18.IV.18 MONT DES CATS Early in the morning the Bde Group was relieved and returned to the MONT DES CATS area, reaching there about 7 a.m. The day was spent resting and cleaning up and towards evening we were joined by 135 reinforcements. MAJ. STEWART rejoined temporarily.
All through the operations it is worthy of note that each night our rations and stores were sent up to us without fail - often under great difficulty. This reflects great credit upon those responsible CAPT. BENNETT, Lt CROTHERS and C.Q.M.S MALLEY and BURROWS and the Transport & Q.M. branch generally.

19.IV.18 Snow fell during the night and training and cleaning up was proceeded with during the day. An unfortunate incident was the bursting of an enemy shell in one of the huts killing 5 and wounding many.
The day was cold and bleak.

Instructions regarding War Diaries and Intelligence Summaries are contained in F. S. Regs., Part II. and the Staff Manual respectively. Title pages will be prepared in manuscript.

WAR DIARY
or
INTELLIGENCE SUMMARY.
(*Erase heading not required.*)

1 Border Regt

Vol 32

Army Form C. 2118.

Place	Date May 1918	Hour	Summary of Events and Information	Remarks and references to Appendices
LA-CLYTTE	1 Wed.		Beyond intermittent shelling the day was very quiet	
	2 Thurs		do. do.	
	3 Friday		About 7-30 pm the Bn moved back out of the lines. On arrival at L16 d 22 (Sheet 27) a hot meal was ready for the men. After one hours halt the Bn again moved back to L29 A 15-20 where they rested for the remainder of the night.	
ST ELOI CABT L29 A 15-20	4 Sat.		The following officers having reported to the Transport lines on 2nd Inst were taken on the strength of the Bn and posted to the Coys shown against their names:-	
			Lt A.L.M. SHEEHAN B Coy	
			" W. BECKETT-DEN D "	
			2nd Lt E.A. JACKSON D "	
			" H.R. SHAWE B "	
			" H.G. MACHELL A "	
			" G.A. SUTCLIFFE C "	
			" A.S. PEARSON D "	
			Lt G.E.H. SLATER A "	
			At 10.30 AM in accordance with Bde instructions the Battalion marched via WATTOU-HOUTKERQUE, HERZEELE to billets in the vicinity of WYLDER. Bn HQ at PONT DE WYLDER. Coys were settled in their billets by 3-30 pm.	

31. N. 14 sheets

A7092). Wt. W12839/M1293 750,000. 1/17. D. D & L., Ltd. Forms/C2118/14.

Instructions regarding War Diaries and Intelligence Summaries are contained in F. S. Regs., Part II. and the Staff Manual respectively. Title pages will be prepared in manuscript.

WAR DIARY
or
~~INTELLIGENCE SUMMARY.~~
(*Erase heading not required.*)

Army Form C. 2118.

Place	Date May 1918	Hour	Summary of Events and Information	Remarks and references to Appendices
WYLDER	5 Sun		Inspection of Billets. Church Service	
	6 Mon		CO's inspection. The remainder of the day was spent in cleaning up & reorganizing. Kit inspections. Medical inspection. And forming new Lewis Gun and Signalling Classes.	
	7 Tues		Physical training and Arms Drill. Lewis Gun and Signalling Classes. Lt V BLOOMFIELD appointed Bn Lewis Gun Officer.	
	8 Wed		Physical training, arms drill and classes. The following officers having reported on joining were posted to Coys as stated against their names:-	
			2nd Lt R SCOTT D Co — 2nd Lt D PHILIP D Co	
			" J K MACKENZIE C " — " J BROWN A "	
			" A HEPBURN B " — " J D DEAS B "	
			" W T THORNTON C " — " L RITCHIE C "	
			" A A R DALLAS A " — " J GORDON A "	
	9 Thur		At 3 AM the Bn marched to entraining point at HEIDEBEKE arriving there at 7 AM. Breakfast was issued and at 10.15 AM the train moved off. The remainder of the day was spent in the train.	
TRAIN	10 Fri		At 8-30 pm the train arrived at the detraining point (FISMES).	
FISMES			The Bn then marched to billets in COURVILLE arriving there at 10 pm.	
	11 Sat		Cleaning up. Kit inspection etc.	

Army Form C. 2118.

WAR DIARY
or
INTELLIGENCE SUMMARY.
(Erase heading not required.)

Instructions regarding War Diaries and Intelligence Summaries are contained in F. S. Regs., Part II. and the Staff Manual respectively. Title pages will be prepared in manuscript.

Place	Date	Hour May 1918	Summary of Events and Information	Remarks and references to Appendices
COURVILLE.	12 Sun		Billet inspection by C.O. Church services	
			Lt M. TURNBULL appointed Bn Signalling Officer. At 5 pm the Bn was	
	~~12 Sun~~		inspected with the other units of the Bde group by the Divisional Commander.	
	13 Mon		Training. Physical Training. Bayonet fighting. Musketry. Squad Drill Gas Drill and Classes.	
	14 Tues		Do. Do.	
	15 Wed		Do. Do.	
			Lt Col J.N. de la PERRELLE DSO MC having arrived took over Command of the Bn.	
			Capt J. DAWSON MC having reported was taken on the strength of the Bn and took over Command of "A" Co.	
	16 Thur		Training. Physical Training. Bayonet Fighting. Musketry. Gas Drill	
	17 Fri		and Classes.	
			Lt A.L.M. SHEEHAM was appointed Bn Signalling Officer vice Lt M. TURNBULL who took over the duties of A/Adjutant.	
	18 Sat		Training	
			2nd Lt F.W. DARVELL appointed Intelligence Officer	
	19 Sun		Church parade and services.	
	20 Mon		Training.	

A7092). Wt. W12839/M1293 750,000. 1/17. D. D & L., Ltd. Forms/C2118/14.

Instructions regarding War Diaries and Intelligence Summaries are contained in F. S. Regs., Part II. and the Staff Manual respectively. Title pages will be prepared in manuscript.

Army Form C. 2118.

WAR DIARY
or
~~INTELLIGENCE SUMMARY.~~
(Erase heading not required.)

Place	Date May 1918	Hour	Summary of Events and Information	Remarks and references to Appendices
COURVILLE	21 Tue		Training including firing 100 yds grouping and 200 yds application.	
	22 Wed		Do	
	23 Thur		Do 2 hrs specialists only.	
			At 7.5 pm the Bn marched to ~~billets in VENTELAY~~ ROMAIN CAMP EAST. 500 yds N of I in ROMAINE arriving in Camp about 11.45 pm.	Ref MAP SOISSONS
ROMAIN CAMP	24 Fri		The morning was spent in cleaning up the Camp. During the afternoon Coys practiced "Coy in the attack" and specialists had their usual instruction.	
			2nd Lt. H LANSLEY reported for duty and was posted to C Coy.	
	25 Sat		Training. Specialists. Coy in the attack. Musketry.	
VENTELAY	26 Sun		Church parade in the morning.	
		6.45pm	At 6.45 pm orders were received from Bde to be prepared to move within one hour.	
		9.30pm	At 9.30pm the Bn moved to a position South of VENTELAY – BOUVANCOURT road about 800 yds E of VENTELAY and there awaited further orders.	
	27 Mon	1 AM	At about 1 AM the Enemy bombardment opened and a few HE and Gas shells fell in our vicinity.	
			Orders were received to reconnoitre roads and approaches to CONCEVREUX, ROUCY and GERNICOURT. [illegible] were sent out.	

A7092). Wt. W12839/M1293 750,000. 1/17. D. D & L., Ltd. Forms/C2118/14.

WAR DIARY

Place	Date May 1918	Hour	Summary of Events
VENTELAY.	27 May	6.35 AM	At 6.35 AM Orders were received to send one platoon per Co to take up position astride VENTELAY–ROUCY road in front of LA PEITS farm [illegible] to Bn taking up that line.
		7.30 AM	At 7.30 AM Orders were received to move forward and take up a position to defend the bridge head at PONTAVERT. This task was allotted to C & D Cos with A–B Cos in support.
		8.30 AM	At 8.30 AM Orders were received to move forward and defend the bridge heads between PONTAVERT and CONCEVREUX. There were eight bridges and dispositions were made so that each Coy held two bridges.
		9.30 AM	At 9.30 AM the Bn moved off. Between VENTELAY and ROUCY information was received that the Enemy were already across the River and Canal. Orders were then received to send two Cos forward at once to reinforce the 2nd SOUTH LANCS in a line 100 yds North of the village of ROUCY to the East of the ROUCY–PONTAVERT road. A & C Cos were sent forward, B & D Cos were ordered to remain in support in the vicinity of ROUCY.
ROUCY.			On arrival at ROUCY at midday B Co was sent forward to reinforce the 11th CHESHIRES on the left of the 2nd SOUTH LANCS and D Co was placed in close support to the 11th CHESHIRES to the West of ROUCY. Bn HQ were established in a [illegible]
		12.30 pm	and immediately behind D Co. At 12.30 pm a message was received from C Co to say they were in position 150 yds South of railway N of ROUCY and later a message from A Co saying

[M1787] W10715/M1107 1000m 12/16s 191 G & S E. 688. Forms/W. 3121/4

Army Form W. 3121.

_______ Brigade. _______ Division. _______ Corps. _______ Date of Recommendation.

Schedule No. (to be left blank)	Unit	Regtl. No.	Rank and Name (Christian names must be stated)	Action for which commended (Date and place of action must be stated)	Recommended by	Honour or Reward	(To be left blank)

WAR DIARY

PLACE	DATE	HOUR	Summary of Events
	May 1918		
Roucy	27 May		they had placed themselves under the 2nd SOUTH LANCS and were occupying the Northern slope of the BUTTE de MARCHANNE.
		1 pm.	At 1 pm orders were received from Brigade to withdraw two Coys into reserve to the top of the hill on the southern outskirts of Roucy. B & D Cos were withdrawn and held in readiness in BOIS de ROUVROY. Each Co sent forward an officer and small party to reconnoitre approaches to position held by 2nd SOUTH LANCS
		2 pm	and at 2 pm one Co was ordered to move forward but the line to the west of BOUFFIGNEREUX. D Co went forward but was unable to advance owing to heavy MG fire and was ordered by the Brigade Major to fall back to their original position. A patrol was then sent out to ascertain the situation on the right and failed to return. The line appeared to have fallen back on the right but could not be located.
		3 pm.	At 3 pm orders were received to move back about 300 yds and take up a position astride the VENTELAY-ROUCY road with our right resting on the BOIS ROUVROY. D Co were placed on the right and B Co on the left of the road.
			Details of the 8th & 50th Divisions were collected and placed in the line on the left also a small party of 11th Cheshires under Capt WILKINSON. A number of MGs were collected and placed for the defence of the position.
			One MG and one LG were placed in a position to command

[M1787] W10715/M1107 1000m 12/16s 191 G & S E. 688. Forms/W. 3121/4

Army Form W. 3121.

________ Brigade. ________ Division. ________ Corps. ________ Date of Recommendation.

Schedule No. (to be left blank)	Unit	Regtl. No.	Rank and Name (Christian names must be stated)	Action for which commended (Date and place of action must be stated)	Recommended by	Honour or Reward	(To be left blank)

WAR DIARY

PLACE	DATE (May 1918)	HOUR	Summary of Events
ROOCY	27 Mon		the road. Lt BLOOMFIELD went forward to the left front with four L.Gs but was forced to fall back on the main line
		4.30pm	At about 4.30pm a number of the Enemy emerged from the wood and rushed down the road cheering and shouting. They were soon repulsed and heavy casualties inflicted. Patrols were then sent out on both flanks but were unable to locate any British troops. Our position was reported to Brigade who told us to hang on. They were arranging to send up ammunition which however did not arrive
		5.30pm	At about 5.30pm the Enemy commenced to encircle our position. He brought up heavy T.Ms and shelled the road and even in front of our position inflicting some casualties. They crawled out from the wood in front and started to snipe. At the same time they advanced through the woods on both flanks and started to enfilade our position with M.G fire. At this point orders were sent to a party of 75th T.M Battery who had been previously ordered to withdraw to Lt FAITE farm [?] owing to come forward and deal with the Enemy M.Gs in the wood. The runners failed to find this party and no more were seen of them
		7. pm.	At about 7pm a Colonel from 8th Divn HQ informed us that a

[M1787] W10715/M1107 1000m 12/16s 191 G & S E. 688. Forms/W. 3121/4

Army Form W. 3121.

________ Brigade. ________ Division. ________ Corps. ________ Date of Recommendation.

Schedule No. (to be left blank)	Unit	Regtl. No.	Rank and Name (Christian names must be stated)	Action for which commended (Date and place of action must be stated)	Recommended by	Honour or Reward	(To be left blank)

Army Form C. 2118

WAR DIARY

Place	Date (May 1918)	Hour	Summary of Events
ROVEY	27 Mon	7 pm	French Regiment was moving up to reinforce us. By this time the position on our right made it imperative for the right flank to swing back. This was successfully done. The left of the line had by this time suffered heavy casualties and part of it on the extreme left consisting of mixed details of various units had broken and withdrawn.
		10.30pm	The Bn continued to hold on to the position until about 10.30pm. By this time the position had become untenable. Enemy were close in the farm 500 yds North of BOURGOGNE and were firing from our left rear. The Bn withdrew to a position
LA PAITE FM			immediately in front of LA PAITE Farm. On arrival at the position an order was received from 23rd Bde to hang on to our line and informing us that a party of 5th CHESHIRES was coming up on our right flank. This party failed to reach us. Two runners were sent back to try and find the location of 23rd Bde HQ but they failed to return. Immediately after taking up the position the enemy fired a Very light from the valley about 600 yds to the N.W. of VENTELAY and numbers of the enemy were seen in the valley. These were dispersed by our rifle and LG fire. A patrol under Cpl ROBINSON was immediately sent out who brought back identification from a wounded enemy. Papers and identification were dispatched to Bde by runner

[M1787] W10715/M1107 1000m 12/16s 191 G & S E. 688. Forms/W. 3121/4

Army Form W. 3121.

________ Brigade. ________ Division. ________ Corps. ________ Date of Recommendation.

Schedule No. (to be left blank)	Unit	Regtl. No.	Rank and Name (Christian names must be stated)	Action for which commended (Date and place of action must be stated)	Recommended by	Honour or Reward	(To be left blank)

Army Form C. 2118.

WAR DIARY

Place	Date May 1918	Hour	Summary of Events	Remarks and references to Appendices
LA PAITE	27 June	11.30pm	who were fired on at from VENTELAY and failed to find Bde HQ. Later two runners were sent back to inform Bde of our exact dispositions but they were unable to get through and brought back information that VENTELAY was in the hands of the Enemy. Lt Col de la PERRELLE and Capt BENTLEY then went out to the west of LA PAITE farm to reconnoitre a position to be occupied before dawn. They were fired on by an Enemy MG and it was apparent that the position was surrounded. After a brief consultation it was decided that an attempt should be made before dawn to break through and rejoin our troops.	
	28 June	1.30AM	About 1.30AM the remaining troops were formed up on the road running through the farm. Advance, flank and rear guards were detailed and the Bn proceeded along the spur running south between VENTELAY and ROMAIN. Our left flank guard became engaged with the Enemy on the outskirts of VENTELAY and the remainder were enabled to get through to ROYAIN which was occupied by 21st French Infantry Regt whose HQ had just moved to BREUIL.	
ROMAIN			The Bn then proceeded to BREUIL and reported to Lt Col WEILLER commanding the 21st I.R. Here information was received that the 75 Inf Bde HQ were at MONTIGNY. On receiving this information the Bn moved to LES VENTEAUX and on arrival there runners were sent out to locate Bde	

[M1787] W10715/M1107 1000m 12/16s 191 G & S E. 688. Forms/W. 3121/4

Army Form W. 3121.

_______ Brigade. _______ Division. _______ Corps. _______ Date of Recommendation.

Schedule No. (to be left blank)	Unit	Regtl. No.	Rank and Name (Christian names must be stated)	Action for which commended (Date and place of action must be stated)	Recommended by	Honour or Reward	(To be left blank)

Army Form W. 3121.

WAR DIARY

Place	Date (May 1918)	Hour	Summary of Events	Remarks and references to Appendices
LES VENTEUX	[illegible]		HQrs and report our progress. These runners failed to return and later two more runners were dispatched who returned with the information that our troops were retiring and that the Bde could not be found.	
COURVILLE			A D.R. was found who said he was looking for Bde. A message was dispatched by him to Bde that we could not find them and were placing ourselves under the Command of the 21st D[illegible] (French). On doing so we were ordered to report to the Officer Commanding 3rd Bn [illegible] at FM. BONNE MAISON on the hill to the NE of COURVILLE. The troops at the disposal of the [illegible] were formed into two Coys. One Company consisting of the Border Regt and the other of details from various Units of the 8th and 50th Divisions. A position was taken up between two French Battalions in the Aerodrome on the high ground N of COURVILLE.	
		2 pm	At 2 pm the Enemy launched a [illegible] attack on our position. The Bn of French on our right gave way and fell back.	
		3 pm	At 3 pm orders were received to occupy a position astride the spur to the North of CRUGNY.	
CRUGNY		5 pm	At 5 pm the Enemy who had been working round our left flank launched an attack from the direction of COURVILLE which appeared to be in his hands.	

[M1787] W10715/M1107 1000m 12/16s 191 G & S E. 688. Forms W. 3121/4

Army Form W. 3121.

__________ Brigade. __________ Division. __________ Corps. __________ Date of Recommendation.

Schedule No. (to be left blank)	Unit	Regtl. No.	Rank and Name (Christian names must be stated)	Action for which commended (Date and place of action must be stated)	Recommended by	Honour or Reward	(To be left blank)

Army Form C. 2118.

WAR DIARY

Place	Date	Hour	Summary of Events
ROMIGNY	29 Wed.	10 pm	About 10 pm the French troops who were occupying the ridge in front of our position fell back to the flank leaving a gap of about 500 yds. This was patrolled continually throughout the night.
	30 Thurs.	4 AM	About 4 AM the Enemy were seen advancing down the slope towards Fm N.W. of [illegible]. They continued to work down the valley and owing to the French withdrawing our left flank was in the air and the village of ROMIGNY undefended from S.W. By this time our position came under heavy Enemy M.G. fire and light field gun fire from the ridge. The troops on our right withdrew leaving our right flank in the air. As our position had become untenable we gradually withdrew in a S.W. direction over the VILLE EN TARDENOIS – ROMIGNY road into the Bois de BENIAL and turning round in a westerly direction took up a position on the front edge of the wood facing North. The position ran along the front of wood from point 800 yds S.W. of ROMIGNY to where track from [illegible] to ROMIGNY – JONQUERY road. By this time the Enemy were in the village of ROMIGNY but were driven out by a counter attack by the N.F.s. Good targets were fired on from our position and we were able to check [illegible] fire.
		10 AM	At 10 AM the wood was very heavily shelled with 4.2 H.E.

[M1787] W10715/M1107 1000m 12/16s 191 G & S E. 688. Forms/W. 3121/4

Army Form W. 3121.

_______ Brigade. _______ Division. _______ Corps. _______ Date of Recommendation.

Schedule No. (to be left blank)	Unit	Regtl. No.	Rank and Name (Christian names must be stated)	Action for which commended (Date and place of action must be stated)	Recommended by	Honour or Reward	(To be left blank)

WAR DIARY

PLACE	May 1918 DATE	HOUR	Summary of Events
LHERY.	June 28	5 pm	Since both flanks of our position were again in the air a withdrawal was ordered to the South of LHERY. By this time ammunition was running short and the French were unable to supply either ammunition or rations we were ordered to the rear to get in touch with our division. The remainder of the Bn proceeded in the direction of BROUILLET coming under heavy enemy shelling from BOULEUSE the Bn marched to LAGERY where rations were waiting but no ammunition
AOUGNY.		9 pm.	At 9 pm we proceeded to AOUGNY and on arrival here rested for a few hours
	29 Wed	4 AM.	At 4 AM we proceeded to ROMIGNY and here reported to 8 Div HQ We received orders to rest in a field 1 mile S of ROMIGNY and await further orders.
ROMIGNY.		10 AM.	At 10 AM in accordance with orders received from 8 Div a position was taken up on the west side of the LHERY–ROMIGNY road about ½ mile from ROMIGNY. On taking up this position we came under the orders of 74 Inf Bde On our left were the 1st Field Coy RE and on our right the 1st CHESHIRES. The position held by us was a reserve line i.e. the enemy broke through from LHERY. Beyond slight shelling the day was fairly quiet.

[M1787] W10715/M1107 1000m 12/16s 191 G & S E. 688. Forms/W. 3121/4

Army Form W. 3121.

________ Brigade. ________ Division. ________ Corps. ________ Date of Recommendation.

Schedule No. (to be left blank)	Unit	Regtl. No.	Rank and Name (Christian names must be stated)	Action for which commended (Date and place of action must be stated)	Recommended by	Honour or Reward	(To be left blank)

WAR DIARY

PLACE	May 1918 DATE	HOUR	Summary of Intelligence
REMIGNY	30 Thurs		Owing to the heavy shelling our line was withdrawn about 200yds. On our right was a Bn of South Wales Borderers. On our left the French.
		6 pm	At 6 pm a Coy of French troops came up and took over the line held by us. Runners were sent out to try and find Bde HQ, but they failed to do so. Orders were then received from the French to take up a position on either side of the VALE EN TARDINOIS – JONQUERY road about 200yds from the rear edge of the wood. The remainder of the night was fairly quiet.
NAPPES	31 Fri	5 AM	At 5 AM in accordance with instructions received from 74 Bde the Bn withdrew to NAPPES and took up a position of readiness on ridge running from CARBON WORKS along North side of road to CHAMBRY. We remained here until
		6 pm	6 pm when orders were received to take up a position running from W side of BOIS de ECLISE for 200 yds towards T in BOUTACOURT. The 1/6 CHESHIRES were on our left flank and 2 HA on our right with details of 74 Bde in support. Posts were dug and patrols were pushed well forward and [illegible] the wood.

[M1787] W10715/M1107 1000m 12/16s 191 G & S E. 688. Forms/W. 3121/4

Army Form W. 3121.

_______ Brigade. _______ Division. _______ Corps. _______ Date of Recommendation.

Schedule No. (to be left blank)	Unit	Regtl. No.	Rank and Name (Christian names must be stated)	Action for which commended (Date and place of action must be stated)	Recommended by	Honour or Reward	(To be left blank)

WAR DIARY

PLACE	DATE	HOUR	Summary of Events
NAPPES	May 1918 31st		About 10pm a message was received from Bde saying that small parties of the Enemy were trickling through from VILLE EN TARDINOIS.
			Lt ROBINSON took out a patrol but encountered no Enemy.
			The remainder of the night was quiet.

Casualties

	Killed	Wounded	Missing
Officers	2nd Lt J. BELL	2nd Lt H W S YOUNG	Capt A MISSCAMPBELL
	J R McKENSIE	" E W JACKSON	Lt H LANSLEY
			2nd Lt W T THORNTON
			" J BROWN
			" D PHILIP
			" C SPENCE
			" F H DARVELL
			" G A SUTCLIFFE
Other ranks	9	60	203.

Honours during Month.

14455	Sgt	GRAHAM H F	MM	15091	Sgt	CRAYSON M	Pon. to H.M.
28895	Pte	HEWITT W	"	15453	Pte	JONES J R	
203133	L/C	BRAY E W	"	203060		TOORILL H	
15047	Pte	GEORGE J	"				
26595	"	JONES W D	"				
14659	"	STAFFORD W J	"				
15754	"	McGUINNESS T	"				

[illegible signature]

Lt Col Comdg
8 Border Regt

[M1787] W10715/M1107 1000m 12/16s 191 G & S E. 688. Forms/W. 3121/4

Army Form W. 3121.

_______________ Brigade. _______________ Division. _______________ Corps. _______________ Date of Recommendation.

Schedule No. (to be left blank)	Unit	Regtl. No.	Rank and Name (Christian names must be stated)	Action for which commended (Date and place of action must be stated)	Recommended by	Honour or Reward	(To be left blank)

WAR DIARY.

POYSER'S Battalion,

(8th Border Regt. & 9th L.N. Lancs.)

June, 1918.

Volume —

25 DIV 175 BDE

25/50

Army Form C. 2118.

50/25

33

Instructions regarding War Diaries and Intelligence Summaries are contained in F. S. Regs., Part II. and the Staff Manual respectively. Title pages will be prepared in manuscript.

WAR DIARY
or
~~INTELLIGENCE SUMMARY.~~

(Erase heading not required.)

8th Bn The Border Regt

Place	Date 1918 June	Hour	Summary of Events and Information	Remarks and references to Appendices
NAPPES	1	4.30AM	Orders were received from Bde to move to South West Corner of BOIS DE ECLISSE and await further orders. The Bn with other details of the 25 Division then became 19th Divisional reserve.	Ref Map SOISSONS
		2pm	Orders were received that a Composite Battalion would be formed. This Battalion was called the 1/25 Divisional Composite Battalion and commanded by Major TRAIL of the 1st Bn Worcestershire Regt. The 8 Border Regt had to supply 4 Officers and all other ranks (104). The following officers were detailed. Lt C. A. SCOTT " V BLOOMFIELD 2Lt J.D DEAS " R SCOTT One Coy was formed and called No 2 Coy (Border Co)	
		6pm	The Border Co proceeded to BOIS DE COURTON where it remained until	
		9pm	9pm. During this time the wood came under heavy shell fire inflicting few casualties. The Company was then moved to BOIS DE ECLISSE where it remained with the Bn in reserve.	
	2	10AM	The Company in conjunction with the remainder of the 1/25th took up a position in support to the French, the Border Company holding a front of 250 yds 500 yds S of CHANTEREINE Fm. The remainder of the day was quiet.	
	3		With the exception of slight shelling during the day nothing important happened. In accordance with orders from 74 Bde 2nd Lt J.D. DEAS went to the 2/25th Divisional Composite Battalion.	

32.N. 4 sheets

D. D. & L., London, E.C. (A8003) Wt. W1771/M2031 750,000 5/17 Sch. 52 Forms/C2118/14

Instructions regarding War Diaries and Intelligence Summaries are contained in F. S. Regs., Part II. and the Staff Manual respectively. Title pages will be prepared in manuscript.

WAR DIARY
or
~~INTELLIGENCE SUMMARY.~~
(*Erase heading not required.*)

Army Form C. 2118.

Place	1918 Date June	Hour	Summary of Events and Information	Remarks and references to Appendices
NAPPES.	3	9 pm	The Battalion took up a position in depth holding the front of CHANTEREINE FM (Southern Corner of BOIS DE ECLISSE) the Border Company lying in close support	
	4		Remained in same position	
	5		Do 2 patrols were sent out.	
	6.	3.15 AM	The Enemy put down a heavy barrage of HE and Gas on the right of our position, which was followed by an attack. The attack was successfully repulsed. Casualties (5 wounded) were inflicted on the Border Co.	
	7.		Same position. The day was very quiet.	
	8		Do	
	9.	10.30 pm.	The Battalion was relieved by the 1/8 Divisional Composite Bn and on completion of relief went into reserve in the BOIS DE COURTON.	
	10.		Resting	
	11		Do	
	12		During the 12th & 13th the Border Company found a working	
	13		party of 1 NCO and 20 men daily.	
	14	9.30 pm	The Bn moved up to the front line and relieved the 2/25 Divisional Composite Bn, the Border Company taking over the front line from CHANTEREINE FM to a point 300 yds west of the L in BOIS DE ECLISSE	
	15		Holding the line.	
	16		Do	
	17		Do	
	18	1.30 am	The Composite Bn was relieved by the 52nd Bn ALPE. Regt. (Italians)	

D. D. & L., London, E.C. (A8001) Wt. W1771/M2031 750,000 5/17 Sch. 52 Forms/C2118/14

Instructions regarding War Diaries and Intelligence Summaries are contained in F. S. Regs., Part II. and the Staff Manual respectively. Title pages will be prepared in manuscript.

WAR DIARY
or
~~INTELLIGENCE SUMMARY.~~
(Erase heading not required.)

Army Form C. 2118.

Place	Date 1918 June	Hour	Summary of Events and Information	Remarks and references to Appendices
NAPPES.	18		and on relief marched to GERMAINE arriving there at 12 30 pm	Ref Map SOISSONS
GERMAINE		3 pm	The Border Company entrained and arrived at FERE CHAMPENOISE at	
		7 30 pm	From here they were conveyed in lorries to St LOUP and rejoined the remainder of the 8th Border Regt	
St LOUP	19		Cleaning up, Bathing &c	Ref Map ARCES
	20		In accordance with instructions received from Bde the Bn detailed 12 Officers and 36 other ranks to form with the remainder of the 9th Loyal North Lancs No 2 Bn of the 50th Divisional Composite Brigade.	
			Two Coys were organised and on completion were handed over with the Transport Section to 9th Loyal North Lancs	
	21		awaiting instructions	
	22		do	
CONNANTRAY	23		The remaining details of the Bn (16 officers and 86 other ranks) marched to CONNANTRAY arriving there at 4 pm	
HAUSSIMONT	24		Marched to HAUSSIMONT arriving there at 1 pm	
	25	11 pm	At 11 pm the Bn along with details of 75 Bde marched to the station at SOMMESOUS where they entrained.	
SOMMESOUS.	26	3.30 am	left the station at 3.30 AM. The train halted at 11.30 AM at MONTEREAU for 45 minutes.	
	27		Travelling. Another halt was made at US-MARINES.	
HESDIN.		1 pm	The train arrived at HESDIN at 1 pm where the Bn detrained and after tea marched to billets at EMBRY arriving there at 9 pm.	Ref Map LENS 11.
EMBRY.	28		Cleaning up,	
	29		The Staff of 25 Division left for England leaving the Bn along with	ABBEVILLE

D. D. & L., London, E.C.
(A8001) Wt. W1771/M2031 750,000 5/17 Sch. 52 Forms/C2118/14

Instructions regarding War Diaries and Intelligence Summaries are contained in F. S. Regs., Part II. and the Staff Manual respectively. Title pages will be prepared in manuscript.

WAR DIARY
or
INTELLIGENCE SUMMARY.
(Erase heading not required.)

Army Form C. 2118.

Place	Date	Hour	Summary of Events and Information	Remarks and references to Appendices
MAP. SOISSONS.	1/6/18.		Battn in support at C in CHARTEREINE – 8 Officers and 39 Other Ranks. At dawn received verbal orders from G.O.C. 74th Infy Brigade, to concentrate on S.W. edge of BOIS d'ECLISSE. Details of 25th Division were formed into 1/25th Composite Battn, under Lt Col TRAILL D.S.O, 3rd Worcester Rgt. This Battn reorganised in N.W. Portion of BOIS de COURTON. Remnants of this unit formed part of No 1. Coy. About 6-0pm the Coy (9th L.N.L.) moved to S.W. edge of BOIS d'ECLISSE in readiness to restore situation on 57th Brigade front.	
	2/6/18.	10am	Orders received to take up position 500 yds S.W of BOIS d'ECLISSE to hold a 500 yds frontage. 50th Composite Battn on right. 1/6th Cheshire details on left. Capt W.S. Hartley very slightly wounded.	
	3/6/18		During evening took up position occupied by 50th Division.	
	4/6/18		No 1 Coy relieved by No 3 Coy, and took up position in slit trenches on ridge 200 N of second E in CHANTEREINE	
	6/6/18	3-15am	Enemy barraged our line and placed a large quantity of gas shells in rear. 2nd Lt H.W. SUMMERSON wounded. – Died of wounds shortly afterwards. 1 OR killed and 3 wounded.	
CHALONS SHEET BEAUNAY	7/6/18		Major K.E. Poyser D.S.O. joined Battn at Transport lines. {Details at Transport lines formed into Comp Battn under Lieut R.C. NEWTH.	
	8/6/18.		Part of Battn still in line. Transport + details at BEAUNAY.	
REUVES.	9/6/18.		Transport + details, under Major K.E. POYSER D.S.O. moved to REUVES. The 74th Brigade congratulated by Major Genl Jackson Commanding 50th Division for their excellent behaviour during enemy attack on May 28th + subsequent days that the 74th Brigade was under command of 50th Division. One Bar to M.C. 3 M.C. 1 D.C.M + 7 M.M's awarded Officers + Other Ranks of Battn.	See App. "A"
	10/6/18.		The Coy in line with 1/25th Comp. Battn. Details (Composite Coy) at Transport Lines at REUVES training.	
	11/6/18		Same as 10th. 1 Officer awarded M.C. in Birthday Honours	

A5834 Wt. W4973/M687 750,000 8/16 D. D. & L. Ltd. Forms/C.2118/13.

Instructions regarding War Diaries and Intelligence Summaries are contained in F. S. Regs., Part II. and the Staff Manual respectively. Title pages will be prepared in manuscript.

WAR DIARY
or
INTELLIGENCE SUMMARY.
(Erase heading not required.)

Army Form C. 2118.

Place	Date	Hour	Summary of Events and Information	Remarks and references to Appendices
REUVES.	13 6/18.		G.O.C. 25th Division inspected Composite Coy at Transport Lines. Major E.O. Underhill, M.C. 3rd Worcester Regt, posted to Battn as 2nd in Command.	[illegible]
	14 6/18		Composite Coy inspected by Commanding Officer.	[illegible]
	15 6/18.		Church Parades, for Composite Coy at Transport ~~Lines~~ Lines.	[illegible]
	16 6/18.		Training of Composite Coy at Transport Lines.	[illegible]
REF. MAP. ARCIS.	17 6/18.		Transport + Composite Coy moved to GAYE. Composite Coy in Line, relieved, + moved to GERMAINE.	[illegible]
GAYE.	18 6/18		The composite Coy of 1/25th Comp Battn (7 Officers + 55 OR's) entrained at GERMAINE, and detrained at FERE-en-CHAMPENOISE, and joined the Composite Coy with the Transport. The Battn was once more intact (at GAYE).	[illegible]
	19 6/18		Reorganising and Training. Major K.E. POYSER D.S.O. in command of Battn. 2 Coys + HQrs – total = 15 Officers. 322 Other Ranks.	[illegible]
St LOUP.	20 6/18.		Battn moved to St LOUP to join 2 Coys of BORDER REGT, plus transport, to form No 2 Battn (afterwards known as POYSER'S BATTN) in SUGDEN'S Bde of 50th Divn. Transport of this unit, under Capt + QM H Padwick M.C., with personnel of 48, joined 11th Lancs Fuslrs. Battn, which formed part of No 1 Battn, of SUGDEN'S Bde. Those personnel extra-regimentally employed, remained with 25th Division, as 25th Division details.	[illegible]
	21 6/18		The Battn. is now disposed as follows – Nos. 1 and 2 Coys – 8th Border Regt. – No's 3 and 4 Coys – 9th L.N.L. Headquarters – 9th L.N.L. Battn thus organized, inspected by Commanding Officer.	[illegible]
	22 6/18		Training. Major E.O. Underhill M.C., joined Battn. as 2nd in Command.	[illegible]
	23 6/18.		Church Services. Inspection of Billets by Commanding Officer. Battn. inspected by G.O.C. 50th Division.	[illegible]
	24 6/18.		Training. Ten Military Medals and one Meritorious Service Medal awarded to Other Ranks of the Battn.	[illegible]

A5834 Wt. W4973/M687 750,000 8/16 D. D. & L. Ltd. Forms/C.2118/13.

Instructions regarding War Diaries and Intelligence Summaries are contained in F. S. Regs., Part II. and the Staff Manual respectively. Title pages will be prepared in manuscript.

WAR DIARY
or
INTELLIGENCE SUMMARY.
(Erase heading not required.)

Army Form C. 2118.

Place	Date	Hour	Summary of Events and Information	Remarks and references to Appendices
St. LOUP.	25/6/18 26/6/18		Training.	J.M.M.
	26/6/18.		Transport moved to FROMENTIERES.	J.M.M.
	27/6/18.		Battn. on Field Range near ALLEMANT. Transport returned to Battn at St LOUP.	J.M.M.
	28/6/18.		Training. G.O.C. presented medal ribbons to Officers and Other Ranks of the Battn.	J.M.M.
	29/6/18.		Training.	J.M.M.
	30/6/18.		Church Services.	J.M.M.
			Total casualties during month:- 1 Officer. killed. 1 OR —"— 1 Officer wounded. 3 OR —"—	J.M.M.

K. E. Rogers Lieut Colonel
Comdg No 2 Battn.

A5834 Wt. W4973/M687 750,000 8/16 D. D. & L. Ltd. Forms/C.2118/13.

Army Form C. 2118.

Instructions regarding War Diaries and Intelligence Summaries are contained in F. S. Regs., Part II. and the Staff Manual respectively. Title pages will be prepared in manuscript.

WAR DIARY
or
~~INTELLIGENCE SUMMARY.~~

(Erase heading not required.)

Place	June Date 1918	Hour	Summary of Events and Information	Remarks and references to Appendices
EMBRY	29		Other details of the Division to await instructions from G.H.Q.	
	30		Church Parade.	
			Casualties during Month. Killed Wounded	
			Officers 2nd Lt H.G. MACHELL (DIED)	
			Other Ranks 15	
			Total 1 15	
			Honours & Awards	
			Lt. R. STRONG 2nd Bar to M.C. — 25618 L/C TATTERSALL J. M.M.	
			Capt. A.J. BENTLEY } Military Cross — 9100 Pte DIXON R. "	
			Lt. J.F. DUGGAN DCM } — 33265 " VAUGHAN H. "	
			" F.L. WILLIAMS } — 27963 " BELL (DCM) T. "	
			2/Lt F.W. DARVELL } — 33913 Cpl ROBINSON (DCM) W. "	
			Capt. M. TURNBULL }	
			5793 RQMS KNIGHT J. M.S.M.	
			CSM J.M.J. GENT D.C.M. — 8526 Sgt WALKER J. "	
			10085 Pte ROBERTS E. Bar to M.M. — 14869 " BERRY J. Mentioned in Despatches	
			13513 " BELL J. M.M.	
			260155 " GELLING W. "	
			13548 " HERD J. "	
			25420 Cpl O'CONNELL J. "	
			33418 L/C WILKIE R. "	
			[illegible signature] Lt Col Comdg 8th Bn The Border Regt.	

www.ingramcontent.com/pod-product-compliance
Lightning Source LLC
Chambersburg PA
CBHW082012220426
43670CB00014B/2608
* 9 7 8 1 4 7 4 5 1 3 6 8 5 *